Dedicated to the loved ones of the editor

For Carolin, Anike and Ferdinand

Karl Michael Popp (ed.)

Best practices for commercial use of open source software

Business models, Processes and Tools for Managing Open Source Software

Impressum

Bibliografische Information der Deutschen Nationalbibliothek

Die Deutsche Nationalbibliothek verzeichnet diese Publikation in der Deutschen Nationalbibliografie; detaillierte bibliografische Daten sind im Internet über http://dnb.d-nb.de abrufbar.

Herstellung und Verlag: Bod - Books on Demand, Norderstedt
Cover design: Goetz Burger, www.plan33.de
ISBN-13: 9783738619096

Disclaimer

Copyright © 2015 Dr. Karl Popp

Table of Contents

1. INTRODUCTION _____ 10

2. BUSINESS MODELS FOR OPEN SOURCE SOFTWARE COMPANIES _____ 13

3. OPEN SOURCE LICENSING AS A PART OF A BUSINESS MODEL _____ 31

4. MERGERS AND ACQUISITIONS: DEALING WITH OPEN SOURCE SOFTWARE IN DUE DILIGENCE _____ 42

5. TOOLS FOR OPEN SOURCE SUCCESS _____ 56

6. CREATING DEVELOPER VALUE FROM OPEN SOURCE SOFTWARE MANAGEMENT _____ 76

7. ADVERTISING _____ 88

8. LITERATURE _____ 97

9. INDEX _____ 100

1.   INTRODUCTION   **10**

1.1   WHO SHOULD READ THIS BOOK?   **10**

1.2   OPEN SOURCE USAGE IN COMMERCIAL SOFTWARE   **10**

1.3   BOOK OVERVIEW   **11**

1.4   A BIG THANK YOU   **11**

2.   BUSINESS MODELS FOR OPEN SOURCE SOFTWARE COMPANIES   **13**

2.1   OPEN SOURCE LICENSES AS A KEY FACTOR FOR THE VARIETY OF BUSINESS MODELS **13**

2.2   SUPPLIERS OF OPEN SOURCE SOFTWARE FOR COMMERCIAL USE   **14**

2.3   OPEN SOURCE BUSINESS MODELS IN DETAIL   **17**
CLASSIFICATION OF OPEN SOURCE BUSINESS MODELS   17
COMMUNITY OPEN SOURCE BUSINESS MODEL   19
COMMERCIAL OPEN SOURCE BUSINESS MODELS   20
COMMERCIAL SERVICES FOR OPEN SOURCE   21
COMMERCIAL LICENSING BUSINESS FOR OPEN SOURCE   22

2.4   REVENUE MODELS OF OPEN SOURCE COMPANIES   **24**

2.5   CUSTOMER VIEW: VALUE OF COMMERCIAL LICENSES FOR OPEN SOURCE SOFTWARE **25**

2.6   LEVERAGING THE OPEN SOURCE COMMUNITY FOR COMMERCIAL PURPOSES   **27**
LEVERAGING THE OPEN SOURCE COMMUNITY AS A SUPPLIER   27
LEVERAGING THE OPEN SOURCE COMMUNITY AS PRODUCT OWNER, MAINTAINER AND
SUPPORTER   29

2.7   LEVERAGING THE COMMUNITY AS SALES CHANNEL   **30**

2.8   SUMMARY AND OUTLOOK   **30**

3. OPEN SOURCE LICENSING AS A PART OF A BUSINESS MODEL   **31**

3.1   BUSINESS MODELS AND LICENSES   **31**

3.2   PROPRIETARY SOFTWARE LICENSES   **32**

3.3   FREE SOFTWARE AND OPEN SOURCE SOFTWARE LICENSES   **33**

3.4   HOW SugarCRM LEVERAGES OPEN SOURCE   **34**

3.5   SUMMARY   **39**

3.6   REFERENCES FOR CHAPTER 3   **40**

4. MERGERS AND ACQUISITIONS: DEALING WITH OPEN SOURCE SOFTWARE IN DUE DILIGENCE   **42**

4.1   INTRODUCTION TO INTELLECTUAL PROPERTY DUE DILIGENCE   **43**

4.2   SOURCES AND USAGE OF INTELLECTUAL PROPERTY RIGHTS IN THE SOFTWARE INDUSTRY   **43**

4.3   COMPREHENSIVE IP DUE DILIGENCE   **46**

     REVIEW OF THE UTILIZATION OF INTELLECTUAL PROPERTY   47

     WHAT THE UTILIZATION MEANS WITH REGARD TO OPEN SOURCE SOFTWARE USED   49

     REVIEW OF OWN INTELLECTUAL PROPERTY AND INTELLECTUAL PROPERTY USED   50

4.4   BEST PRACTICE FOR OPEN SOURCE REVIEW IN IP DUE DILIGENCE   **52**

5. TOOLS FOR OPEN SOURCE SUCCESS   **56**

5.1   OPEN SOURCE STRATEGY   **57**

     BUILDING OSS   58

     BUILDING WITH OSS   58

     BUILDING FOR OSS   58

     BUILDING ON OSS   58

5.2   OPEN SOURCE GOVERNANCE   **59**

THE NEED FOR GOVERNANCE   59

5.3   **OPEN SOURCE POLICY AND PROCEDURES**   **60**

5.4   **OPEN SOURCE LOGISTICS – AUTOMATING GOVERNANCE**   **62**

TYPES OF GOVERNANCE TOOLS   63

GOVERNANCE TOOLS – BLACK DUCK OFFERINGS   64

OTHER OPEN SOURCE GOVERNANCE TOOLS   73

6.   **CREATING DEVELOPER VALUE FROM OPEN SOURCE SOFTWARE MANAGEMENT**   **76**

6.1   **HOW COMPANIES MANAGE OPEN SOURCE COMPONENTS AS PART OF SOFTWARE PRODUCTS**   **76**

6.2   **WHAT IS THE IMPACT OF USING "OLD" VERSIONS OF OPEN SOURCE COMPONENTS?** **78**

MISSING BUG FIXES   79

MISSING SECURITY VULNERABILITY FIXES   79

DEPENDENCIES AND POTENTIAL INCOMPATIBILITIES   79

6.3   **CREATING VALUE FOR DEVELOPERS BY CONTINUOUSLY UPDATING OPEN SOURCE COMPONENTS**   **80**

KEY VALUE PROPOSITIONS OF VERSIONEYE   81

DISPLAY OF SECURITY VULNERABILITIES   83

LEVERAGING LICENSE WHITELISTS   83

ACTIVELY MANAGING DEPENDENCIES   84

COVERAGE OF OPEN SOURCE PROJECTS   85

VALUE OF ADDITIONAL INFORMATION ABOUT OPEN SOURCE   87

6.4   **SUMMARY**   **87**

7.   **ADVERTISING**   **88**

7.1   **BOOK: MERGERS AND ACQUISITIONS IN THE SOFTWARE INDUSTRY**   **88**

7.2   **BOOK: INTELLECTUAL PROPERTY MODULARITY IN SOFTWARE PRODUCTS AND SOFTWARE PLATFORM ECOSYSTEMS**   **89**

7.3	**BOOK: PROFIT FROM SOFTWARE ECOSYSTEMS**	**90**
7.4	**OPEN SOURCE BEST PRACTICES WEBSITE**	**91**
7.5	**WWW.DRKARLPOPP.COM WEBSITE**	**92**
7.1	**BOOK: PARTNERING WITH SAP**	**93**
8.	**LITERATURE**	**97**
9.	**INDEX**	**100**

1. Introduction

1.1 Who should read this book?

This book was written by practitioners and consultants for professionals in the software business like executives, business developers, product managers, architects, developers, development operations managers and students to get acquainted and proficient in using open source products in commercial software. But also attorneys might find some of the insights in this book interesting. The high value information in this book can be accessed in different ways. You can browse by chapters or you can use our comprehensive Index in chapter 9 for direct access to topics of interest.

1.2 Open source usage in commercial software

In the software industry there is a lot of activity around open source, like investments in open source projects like Apache and open source companies like Jaspersoft or Red Hat as well as increasing use of open source software overall [1][2].

For a commercial software company, open source software is either software that is licensed to that company under an open source license or software that is provided by that company to customers under an open source license [3], [4]. Accepting the co-existence of open source software and commercial software, the question arises how software vendors leverage open source in their strategies, business models, processes and products.

This book provides an overview of the business models, the processes and tools relevant for commercial software vendors leveraging open source software and open source communities, no matter if the company participates in open source development or not.

1.3 Book overview

Chapters 2 and 3 of this book focus on business model impact of open source products and open source licenses. Chapter 2 gives an overview of the different types of business models for open source companies. Chapter 3, provided by Dr. Josef Waltl, shows how open source licenses and intellectual property strategies can create a unique business model based on a combination of open source and proprietary software.

The next chapter focuses on detection and license compliance aspects of open source software in commercial products. Investments in a software vendor or the acquisition of a software vendor is a typical event to trigger the review of open source license compliance as described by Dr. Karl Michael Popp.

The next two chapters cover the offerings of tool vendors for governance of open source software but also for development enablement. Chapter 5, provided by Bill Weinberg and Greg Olsen, shows the broad offering of solutions of Black Duck Software, a provider for open source governance and enablement tools.

Chapter 6, provided by VersionEye, focuses on development aspects of using open source software as part of commercial products like assistance for developers in selection and in continuously updating open source components during the software development lifecycle.

Please follow the editor on twitter @karl_popp and keep yourself updated via http://opensourcebestpractices.net

1.4 A big thank you

Dear reader, as the editor of this book, I would like to thank you for buying this book. Many people have helped in gathering the knowledge that is the foundation of this book. First and foremost, I would like to thank my colleagues in the SAP corporate development team. In addition I would like to thank my colleagues from the Global Licensing department at SAP SE for working with me on open source related due diligence activities. I am also grateful for the many ideas and inputs that came from discussions at the BDH IP Management Summit located at the House of IT in Darmstadt, Germany.

Also, many thanks go to the authors who have contributed to this book; Dr. Josef Waltl for chapter 3 as well as Bill Weinberg and Greg Olsen for chapter 5 and the people from VersionEye for chapter 6.

I would like to thank partners and sponsors who have supported this book: Black Duck Software and VersionEye.

In addition, cudos go to Ralf Meyer of Synomic, one of the finest consulting companies for software companies. Ralf is a great supporter of my work and has offered to make this book part of the Synomic academy series of books. For more information on the academy, please visit http://www.synomic.com/synomic-academy/

Last but not least I would like to thank my wonderful family and my friends for supporting me in this effort.

Dr. Karl Michael Popp

@karl_popp on twitter

2. Business Models for open source software companies

Dr. Karl Michael Popp, SAP SE

In this chapter, we look at different business models for companies, that base their business model completely or in part on open source software or open source licenses.

2.1 Open source licenses as a key factor for the variety of business models

An open source license comes with rights and obligations and the search for the optimal license continues [1], [3]. A license creates limitations as well as opportunities in creating business models around open source software.

For example, for a company using open source software as part of its products, the limitations can be described as follows.

Example

A software vendor may make use of the rights, like usage or redistribution of the open source, but it also has to fulfill the obligations, like e.g. delivering the copy of the license text with the software or revealing the source code of a software product.

Another restriction is that some licenses do not allow modifications of the open source software. This would exclude the ability of a commercial open source company to provide maintenance, because the open source code must not be changed.

But the limitations of open source licenses can also be an advantage for software vendors providing open source software, which will be shown later in this chapter, when we talk about dual licensing models.

The key point for a commercial company is if it is willing and able to comply with the license terms of a specific open source component. The rights and obligations in conjunction with the open source software have to be analyzed diligently to make sure there is no violation of the license terms and the license terms are not in conflict with the commercial company´s business model [4], [5]. If this is ensured, the company can leverage this piece of open source software.

2.2 Suppliers of open source software for commercial use

Often, open source software is being supplied by a community or by a commercial company [6]. We speak of **community open source** and **commercial open source** respectively.

Community involvement with open source products means that a community of people provides creation, maintenance and support for an open source software [7]. Sometimes the community even provides presales and sales activities for companies offering an open source version and a commercial version of their software. In most of the cases the community provides these services free of charge.

By providing an open source licensed version of a product, a software vendor has the opportunity to outsource certain activities, like development, maintenance and support to the community [8].

Open Source Business Model variations

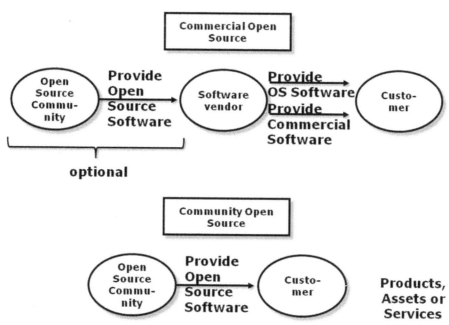

Figure 1: Types of Open Source

There are, of course, differences between a company and the open source community in providing open source software. These differences are important to understand, because they influence a customer's software license selection and they also create niches for companies to establish a business. The differences are listed in Figure 2.

Looking at licenses, community open source usually comes with a single type of license and standard terms. If a commercial company would like to have changes of the license, it is usually not possible to change the license terms with a community. Commercial open source has the advantage that a commercial company issues the license. A software vendor willing to change terms can get in contact and start negotiations of the license terms with that commercial company.

Community vs. Commercial Open Source

	Community Open Source	Commercial open source
License	Open source license, standard terms only	Commercial license, customized terms possible
Consulting	Some help by community, free of charge	Paid consulting services to customer needs
Maintenance	Community provides new versions	Paid maintenance to customer needs
Support	Community supports without guaranteed service level agreements	Paid support to customer needs with guaranteed service level agreements

Figure 2: Commercial open source vs. community open source

Consulting for community open source might come from the community itself or from companies who have specialized on providing commercial consulting for community open source software.

Maintenance for community open source is provided by the community only. While this is free of charge, there is no way to enforce changes and updates of the software. A software vendor using the community open source can escape this issue by donating a source code change to the open source community. This should be a well considered decision, because the software vendor might be giving up intellectual property rights for that change.

Looking at support, a community provides support without guaranteed service level agreements, which is a big issue for commercial companies using that open source software. In commercial open source, there usually is a support offering by the software vendor granting the commercial open source license. In addition, there is often the option to choose a commercial license for the open source software, too, which might come with a commercial support offering.

2.3   Open source business models in detail

Now let us have a more detailed look at the different open source business models.

Classification of open source business models

Based on a general classification of business models [9] we will have a look at open source business models. The following section arguments along the lines of [6].

Figure 3 shows a classification of generic business models. The business models relevant for commercial open source business are marked in bold. In this general classification of business models, software classifies as an intangible product, see the corresponding column "Intangible" in Figure 3.

Software can be created or written ("Inventor"), distributed ("IP Distributor") or licensed or rented to customers ("IP Lessor"). In addition, the customer needs services to run and maintain the software, like implementation, support and maintenance services. These classify as "Contractor" business [6]. We assume here that all open source businesses make use of at least a subset of these four business models. No matter if it is a community or a commercial software vendor, one or many of these business models are applied. By choosing a specific selection of business models, a so-called **hybrid business model** is created. Creating a hybrid business model means combining different business models with their specific goals, requirements and cost structures.

Since these business models are models on a type level, there might be different implementations of how a certain business model is run. An open source community might run the Inventor business for creating software in a different way (leveraging the community) than a commercial software vendor (leveraging a proprietary development team), from a process as well as from a resource perspective. But on a type level, both run the same type of business called Inventor.

Commercial Open Source Business Model

	Type of Products/Services offered			
	Financial	Physical	Intangible	Human
Creator	Entrepreneur	Manufacturer	Inventor	n/a
Distributor	Financial trader	Wholesaler, Retailer	IP distributor	n/a
Lessor	Financial lessor	Physical lessor	IP lessor	Contractor
Broker	Financial broker	Physical broker	IP broker	HR broker

The Software Industry

Ecosystems | Business Models | Partnerships

Figure 3: Commercial open source business model

It is important to note that business model type level and business implementation level are design dimensions for describing existing and designing new open source business models [10]. So creating a new open source business might start with selecting one or more type level business models and then select from existing or new implementations for each of the business models to create a business.

Going forward, we will analyze existing commercial and community open source business models as a selection of a subset of the business models identified here: Inventor, IP Lessor, IP distributor and Contractor.

Community open source business model

The open source community business model usually makes use of the following business models: Inventor, IP Lessor and Contractor.

For the community, the **Inventor business** is what the community is most involved in. It is about creating open source software and engaging with the community members to coordinate the work and collect the contributions of the community members.

The **IP Lessor business** is also important for the community. The IP lessor business defines the terms and conditions of the open source license and makes the software available to customers. The license is defined by the community and all customers using the software have to comply with it. In some cases, there are multiple different licenses for an open source software that a customer can choose from.

The **Contractor** business contains all human services to customers. The community typically provides these via email and they contain services like maintenance, support, translation for country specific versions and the like. They are all carried out by community members. In almost every case, the customer does not pay for these services, but the customer has no rights to enforce any of these services and he does not have service level agreements, like a definition of minimum answer time for support incidents.

The community can serve two types of customers: software vendors and (end) customers. For software vendors, the open source community works as a supplier of software, for the customer, the open source community works as a software vendor licensing software to the customer.

These two relationships differ in the way that customers and software vendors might make use of the software. Customers usually license the software for internal use only. Software vendors license software for internal use and/or for distribution to customers. Often open source software is included in commercial software and provided to customers by the software vendor. In this case, the software vendor has to make sure he complies with all licenses of all open source software he is including in his software product.

Commercial open source business models

In the last section we described the community business model, now we turn to the commercial open source business model. As mentioned before, a commercial software vendor does not have to implement all of these business models, but can rather build a unique business model by selecting a subset of available business models. One basic difference to community open source is that the IP Distributor business model is an option for commercial companies.

The history of commercial open source companies shows that in the beginning the companies focused on services around open source software, which matches the Contractor business. The next step was to build distributions for open source software, like e.g. for Linux. This matches to the IP Distributor business model.

Today, we find all kinds of hybrid business models around open source. Companies are building software and donate it, completely or partially to the open source community (Inventor business model) [11]. Commercial software vendors often package or change or extend existing community open source software, so the community acts as a supplier of open source software to the software vendor. In some cases the software vendor does not use existing open source software from a community, but chooses to offer its proprietary software under a dual licensing strategy, e.g. under a commercial and an open source license.

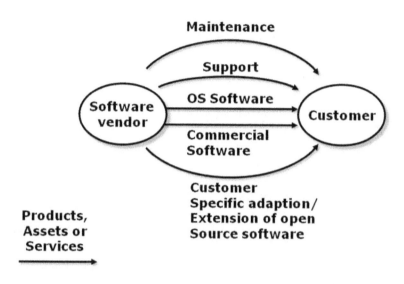

Figure 4: Commercial open source business model

Please note that there are at least two delivery models for open source software: either the software is distributed to the customer and run at the customer's site or the software is provided in a hosted/on demand delivery model.

Commercial services for open source

Since open source licenses are free of charge, many commercial companies first and foremost focused on providing services around open source software [10]. The expectation was simply that customers would still need services and since the license was free, that customers would have more money to spend on services.

Commercial open source companies provide the following services for open source software: Hosting, Maintenance, Support, Consulting and Extension or adaption of open source software to a customer's needs.

Hosting services mean providing hardware and access to that hardware running open source software. Maintenance services consist of the following activities: building future versions, bug fixes and upgrades and providing them to the customers. Support services contain of accepting, maintaining and resolving incidents that the customer has while using the software. Consulting services mean planning and executing the installation and go-live of customers' system landscapes containing the software.

Extension or adaption of open source software based on customer's requests is designing, programming, testing and delivering open source software that has been modified or expanded. Examples for extensions and modifications are:

❏ Functional Extensions for open source applications with country-specific functionality or customer specific functionality;

❏ Extending the usage scenarios for open source to additional countries by adding additional translations of user interfaces;

❏ Adapting open source software, e.g. to make modifications of open source software to run on a currently unsupported hardware platforms.

Commercial licensing business for open source

In the industry, we see three ways how commercial open source companies offer software to customers executing the IP Lessor business model:

❏ Offer or redistribute open source software only, no commercial software offered. In this case, the software vendor needs a hybrid business model containing one or more revenue streams to fund the open source business.

❐ Offer identical products under two licenses (dual license model) [12].

❐ Offer different versions of the same product under two licenses to customers (dual product model).

Multiproduct and multilicense strategies for open source	Single product	Dual products
Single License	„classic case" of Open source license only or of commercial license only	Dual product strategy (market segmentation by product and license)
Dual License (commercial & open source)	Dual license strategy for identical product (customer segmentation by license)	Dual product strategy (market segmentation by product and license)
Dual License (two open source licenses)	Dual license strategy for license compatibility (usage segmentation by license, more usages are possible)	Dual product strategy

Figure 5: Multiproduct and multilicensing strategy for open source.

For a commercial open source company, there are two choices for dual licensing, dual license strategy for identical products or dual product strategy with dual licenses.

Dual license for identical products

Following the **dual license strategy for identical products** [12] a commercial open source company would offer the same product under an open source license and a commercial license. There are good reasons for the company and customers alike to have the choice between the two licenses As mentioned earlier, customers could choose the commercial license for several reasons, like to ensure they get support service level agreements, warranty or liability from the software vendor. The commercial open source software vendor could use a license that does not allow commercial use of the open source software to force commercial users to buy a commercial license.

Dual product with dual licensing

In the **strategy dual product with dual licensing**, the software vendor usually applies versioning. This could mean that a product with limited functionality can be licensed under an open source license and the full product is available under a commercial license.

There are basically two examples for this strategy, freemium [13], [14] and customer specific version of open source under commercial license. Freemium in the context of open source means that a free version of a product under an open source license exists with restrictions compared to a commercial version of the product, like e. g. a reduced set of functionalities. The customer has to pay a premium, a commercial license fee, to get the full version of the product.

2.4   Revenue models of open source companies

The key question for each open source company is: how do they make money? Since there is usually no license revenue or very limited license revenue, there have to be other revenue streams that keep the company alive. This means that a hybrid commercial open source business model combines free-of-charge services and products with services and products that are being charged for.

Relating to Figure 6, there might be a revenue stream for each of the products and services provided for customers.

Commercial Open Source Revenue Model

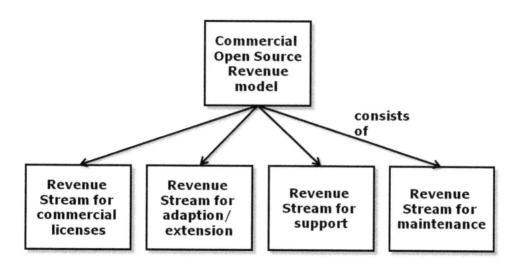

Figure 6: Commercial open source revenue model

In addition to the revenue streams shown, some open source companies use other services to create revenues, like certification and compliance testing, hardware sales and advertising.

In creating the operations plan for the company you have to make sure that the sum of the planned revenue of all revenue streams is big enough to sustain as a profitable company in the long term.

2.5 Customer view: Value of commercial licenses for open source software

Commercial open source vendors offer open source licensed software to their customers. There are different ways software vendors can add value to the open source software like:

- ❏ By packaging [15]: the software vendor creates a distribution by shrinkwrapping open source software and distributes that to the customers (IP distributor business model). The customer can rely on the professional configuration of the package and does not have to have expert knowledge on open source.

- ❏ By providing a commercial license [16] with significant differences to the open source license, like warranty and liability, no copyleft effect, clearly stated usage scenarios of the software and others. So the customer gets some license (or contract) terms that he could not get in the open source license.

- ❏ By creating customer specific adaption or integration of open source software as commercial software. When a customer needs Perl on an exotic hardware platform with 64 bit support, he will contact a company that is specialized in this business and order that specific adaption of the open source software under a commercial license.

- ❏ By omitting advertising in the commercial version of the software while the open source software is containing advertising.

- ❏ By providing better service level agreements, more storage space or other features for a higher service fee. This case applies for open source software in a hosted or on demand delivery model.

But even without the extra value a customer might decide against an open source license and in favor of commercial open source. This is the case, if e.g. a customer needs customized license terms, runs open source in a mission-critical environment and thus needs service level agreements for support or if he needs maintenance provided in a different way than via the open source community. In many business contexts it makes also sense to have liability and warranty provisions from a supplier when using open source. In most of the existing open source licenses there is exclusion of any warranty or liability [3]. This is another reason why companies might choose commercial open source over community open source.

2.6 Leveraging the open source community for commercial purposes

Besides providing open source software to customers, software companies can leverage open source software and the corresponding open source community for their business in the following ways [6]:

☐ Leverage the open source community as supplier, as development resource, marketing, presales, sales, maintenance or support resource.

☐ Leveraging the open source community as product owner, maintainer and supporter and

☐ Leveraging the open source community as sales channel.

To create a commercial open source business model, software companies choose one or several of these levers. This is why there is no single open source business model out there. Let us look closer at the different advantages of a commercial open source model.

Leveraging the open source community as a supplier

Software vendors often use the open source community as a supplier of software. Almost any commercial software on the market contains components that are under an open source license or the solutions use open source software as a runtime environment.

The main reasons to use open source "as supplied material" are quality and cost advantages. Quality advantages have been shown by several studies in the following way: open source software with a community of significant size has a higher quality than similar commercial software.

Regarding cost advantages: If the community is inventing the software, it carries the cost of development. There is no sunk cost for a company to develop the software.

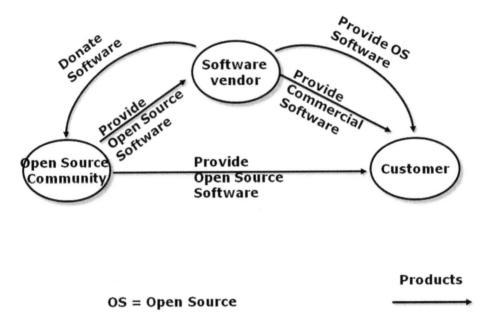

Figure 7: Flow of open source products in a commercial setting

So for the software vendor, the value of open source software is that it comes for free and it provides a significant cost advantage compared to programming a similar, proprietary functionality from scratch. The software vendor might also include and ship the open source software with its solutions. As mentioned before, there is no license fee paid from the software vendor to the open source community. As every open source software comes with license terms, the software vendor has to comply with the license terms of the open source software used [17].

If the software vendor ships the open source software, the software vendor is responsible for support and maintenance of the software shipped, which includes the open source software. So the software vendor has to make sure he is able to maintain and support the open source software.

Since compliance with the license terms of open source software is important, help for doing that is available. There are companies specialized on analyzing open source usage and on analyzing the attached license terms. They offer tools that automatically analyze the source code and determine the list of open source software components used. With this list you can determine if you can comply with the license terms and if you want to continue to use the open source software. See chapters 5 and 6 of this book for more information.

Leveraging the open source community as product owner, maintainer and supporter

The software vendor might decide to donate the source code to the community and let the community drive the product innovation as well as maintenance activities. By doing that, the software vendor further lowers its cost to develop and maintain software.

Commercial software vendors might have different reasons for donating software to the open source community, e.g.:

☐ To create visibility of a software company´s expertise. This is especially interesting for small companies to gain visibility and reputation within a larger community of subject matter experts.

☐ To get rid of the cost for product development, maintenance and support if a product is in the late stages of the product lifecycle or if the product is commoditized or did not create enough revenue.

But how do you make the community owner of a product? You donate proprietary software to the community and make it open source. The following picture shows the flow of products. From this point in time, you lose some control over the product and trade this for the cost saved and the innovation speed of the product.

At the same time, if the community is big enough and active, the quality of the software increases. There is also a good chance that the community, due to its heterogeneity, is a better breeding ground for evolutionary innovation of the product.

2.7   Leveraging the community as sales channel

Software vendors might leverage the community to endorse products via viral marketing. It works like this: community members like the software and endorse its use (at companies). The companies can choose between the open source and the commercial license of the software. If it chooses the commercial license, it will be provided by the software vendor.

Depending on the open source license chosen, the software vendor can force customers into a commercial license for commercial use. This is the case for open source licenses, which do not allow commercial use of the software under the open source license. Another case is the customer wanting to do proprietary changes on the software and keep the ownership of the software, which conflicts with copyleft licenses. Copyleft licenses enforce that all versions, including modified and extended versions, are available for free to the community.

2.8   Summary and outlook

In this section it was shown that a framework exists that can be used to describe business models and that these business models can be combined to create different hybrid business models of commercial open source companies. In addition, an overview was given, how commercial open source companies leverage open source communities for their purposes.

The evolution of open source business and commercial open source business is still underway. We will see, which new hybrid business models will be created in the future, just like the ones we recently saw in open source on demand applications or open source software in cloud environments.

3. Open source licensing as a part of a business model

Dr. Josef Waltl, Amazon Web Services

This chapter explains how the open source licensing strategy can impact the business model of software companies and vice versa. This mechanism is presented in the case of SugarCRM Inc. that built their whole business model around a specific type of hybrid licensing strategy (Waltl *et al.*, 2012).

3.1 Business models and licenses

In general a business model describes how a company creates and appropriates value (Weill et al., 2005; Popp, 2011). Osterwalder (2004) describes a business model as

"a business model is a representation of how a company buys and sells goods and services and earns money".

A business model can be described in a two dimensional topology (Weill *et al.*, 2005; Popp, 2011). The first dimension differentiates the type of right that is being sold. This leads to four basic business models: *creator, distributor, lessor* and the *broker*. While the creator builds goods from basic material and components, the distributor buys goods and sells them. Finally, the lessor sells the allowance to use a good (but not the good itself) and the broker connects sellers and the buyers (Weill *et al.*, 2005; Popp, 2011).

The second dimension distinguishes between the types of assets that are involved which can be: *financial, physical, intangible* or *human services*.

By combining types of goods and services and basic business model types, Weill *et al.* (2005) and Popp (2011) identify 14 specific business model types:

Types of goods/services offered				
	Financial	**Physical**	**Intangible**	**Human**
Creator	Entrepreneur	Manufacturer	Inventor	n/a
Distributor	Financial trader	Wholesaler, retailer	IP distributor	n/a
Lessor	Financial lessor	Physical lessor	IP lessor	Contractor
Broker	Financial broker	Physical broker	IP broker	HR broker

Figure 8: Business model types (Popp, 2011)

Most software product companies[1] focus on the intangible column and implement a business model where the IP lessor business model type funds the inventor business model type (Popp, 2011). The successful implementation of this business model approach depends on the license under which a software product company allows others to use the created Intellectual Property (IP). This license describes what the user of a software product is entitled to do with it (Lindman *et al.*, 2011). We differentiate between *proprietary software licenses and free* and *open source software licenses* (FOSS) (Carver, 2005).

3.2   Proprietary software licenses

In the first case of a traditional proprietary license, the firm charges fees for the use of its software as an IP lessor (Hecker, 1999). The conditions are described in the license terms such as the usage conditions or the number of allowed installations. These licenses are individual contracts between the buyer and the seller and are therefore not standardized. It is also typical that the product is provided in a way that hides the source code to protect the IP of the lessor. Thus, a proprietary software license is the easiest way to appropriate value from existing IP (Riehle, 2012).

---

[1] Here, we refer to the predominant business of software companies to sell products – Software as a Product (SaaP). However, software companies do also sell consulting services and sell software as web services – Software as a Service (SaaS) Popp (2011).

3.3 Free software and open source software licenses

FOSS licenses can be differentiated between *permissive* and *restrictive* (also named copyleft) licenses. Permissive licenses do not require a software company or an individual to reveal the source code for derivative work. The most commonly known permissive licenses are the Massachusetts Institute of Technology (MIT), Berkeley Software Distribution (BSD) and Apache licenses (Lindman *et al.*, 2011). Restrictive licenses such as the GNU General Public License (GPL) require the software company or the individual to publish the final product's source code and to license all derivative work under the same license (Lindman *et al.*, 2011,)[2]. Figure 9 provides an overview of the described software licensing possibilities:

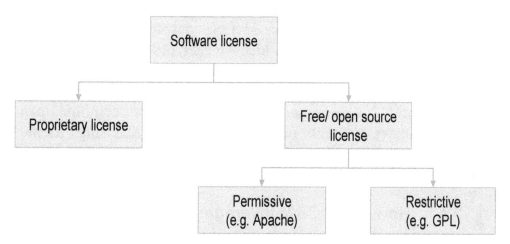

Figure 9: IP lessor compatible software licenses

If an OSS project is implemented as community open source software based on a restrictive license with code coming from a large number of contributors, the potential for distributed value creation is maximized. The downside is that in this case, a product-based business model is

---

[2] The GPL is the most restrictive license. Please refer to www.opensource.org for less restrictive FOSS licenses.

difficult to implement, and the original owner of the code may even lose control over its further development if he does not have the complete copyright for the source code. To overcome these difficulties many companies with a community open source approach generate revenue from OSS related services (Hecker, 1999; Bonaccorsi *et al.*, 2006) which corresponds with the contractor business model shown in Figure 8.

Many firms struggle to combine distributed value creation through an open community and appropriating value out of it. If an OSS project is organized on a public platform, with code coming from a large number of contributors, then the potential for distributed value creation is maximized. Downsides are that in such a case a product-based business model is difficult or impossible, and the original owner of the code may even lose control over its further development.

Various approaches have been proposed, and implemented in practice, to harness the power of community-based OSS development while still running a product-based business model. Hecker (1999) and Raymond (2011) suggest various ways to profit indirectly from OSS, by selling complements. West (2003), Bonaccorsi et al. (2006) and Lindman et al. (2011) study "hybrid" business models empirically, which combine open source and proprietary elements or make use of dual licensing. Riehle (2012) comprehensively presents the properties of this hybrid approach referred to as "single vendor commercial open source business model"[3].

3.4   How SugarCRM leverages open source

An interesting solution to this dilemma provides the company SugarCRM Inc. The firm licenses a community edition of its software under an open source license while selling the commercial edition under a standard proprietary license. However, their approach goes beyond simple dual licensing by creating two distinct versions out of the same code tree.

---

[3] Industry experts also refer to this type of business model as "open core" approach: http://alampitt.typepad.com/lampitt_or_leave_it/2008/08/open-core-licen.html

SugarCRM Inc. was founded in 2004 and provides an open source Customer Relationship Management (CRM) software platform product as well as commercial editions with extended functionality. The business model built around it differs from that of other open source companies in how IP and source code ownership are managed. The company maintains all source code for its products in one proprietary code tree and licenses parts of it for the open source community edition, under the GNU Affero General Public License (see www.gnu.org/licenses). The commercial product editions are sold to customers under proprietary license terms[4]. So SugarCRM combines an open source approach with a proprietary software product business model.

SugarCRM also opened up the platform to enable complementors to create additional extension modules for end-users and build-up a whole software ecosystem.

SugarCRM's platform architecture, the FOSS licensing strategy and its business model are inseparably linked. The business model is enabled by a product architecture that separates the IP elements for the community edition from the elements required for the commercial editions. Figure 10 depicts the basic architecture in an schematic representation for selected platform functionality and extension modules.

---

[4]   Sugar CRM is implemented in PHP technology, which does not allow to keep source code secret for it is interpreted at runtime and not compiled. Following this technical conditions SugarCRM operates on a combination of Open Source Software (OSS) and open code software.

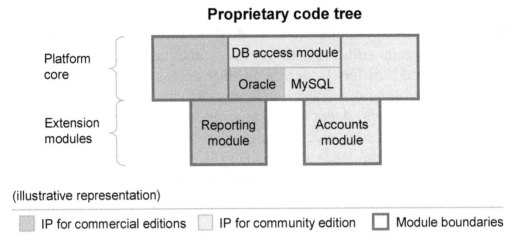

(illustrative representation)

| IP for commercial editions | IP for community edition | Module boundaries |

Figure 10: Schematic Architecture Overview

The goal of SugarCRM is to reach clear modular separation between the open platform core and the extension modules. This is the case when a certain business functionality that is to be included into one of the commercial editions can be fully implemented in one extension module.

However, if this is not possible for some cases, since some functionalities for the commercial edition cannot solely be implemented in an extension module, but also require modifications in the platform core. If possible, such functionality for commercial editions is then encapsulated in separate modules within the platform. In the worst case, the code for the commercial editions cannot be split into different modules within the platform as named components.

To overcome this problem and reach IP homogeneity in the released editions, the code is tagged in the proprietary code tree when it is only to be included in one of the proprietary editions. As shown in Figure 11 a special build process takes out the IP for the commercial editions from the code that is released under the AGPL license. So IP homogeneity within the community and the commercial editions can be achieved with only one proprietary code tree that has to be managed. Alternatively two parallel code trees would have to be managed that only differ in the parts for the commercial editions. This would require additional maintenance effort and increase the risk of incompatibility between the versions.

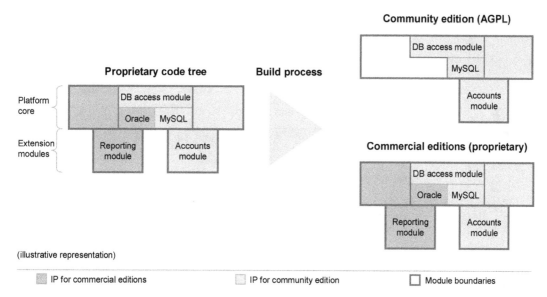

Figure 11: Build process to separate modules with different licenses

Besides enabling SugarCRM's business model, the software license based platform design entails a whole set of additional effects on company performance and the entire platform ecosystem, as depicted in Figure 12.

Within intra-platform effects, it can be further split between effects that increase the platform attractiveness for complementors and those that increase the product attractiveness for end users. Not surprisingly and in line with existing research, the data indicate a network effect between those two. SugarCRM's executives devote particular attention to the platform attractiveness for ecosystem partners, as Chief Marketing Officer Nick Halsey testifies:

> *"By taking the modular architecture approach, we have made it easier for our partner ecosystem to develop add-ons and extensions to our product that they can build businesses around. As a result, that means we have a much larger ecosystem with better solutions that are easier to implement and upgrade."*

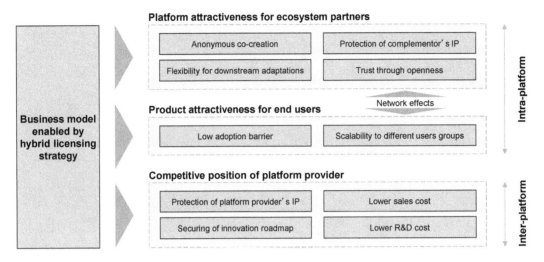

Figure 12: Intra- and inter-platform effects

Furthermore the specific licensing strategy as well as the platform architecture eliminate the need for complementors to directly interact with the platform provider. CEO, Larry Augustin, illustrates why this fosters innovation in the entire ecosystem:

> *"There are many third parties that show up and say: We have a product that works with SugarCRM, and they try to sell to our customer base. Many third parties created those integrations using our open source tools, and they don't have to talk to us at all to develop a useful solution. We may not have supported them if they had chosen to talk to us."*

In addition the low entry barrier and the possibility for anonymous co-creation paved the way for strong partnerships with complementors. Mirco Müller, CEO of InsignioCRM (one of SugarCRM's largest partners in Europe) describes this process as follows:

> *"In the beginning we did our business only based on the community edition. SugarCRM did not know us. We started to partner when we acquired our first big customers – still we did not interact much with SugarCRM. We were able to solve our problems on our own since we had access to all source code for the community and commercial*

editions. That changed when Sugar opened an office in Europe and we now do interact very closely, especially in marketing."

Also, the ecosystem partners appreciate the flexibility for adoption and customization on the platform core to implement end-customer requirements. The core benefits were best described by Clemens von Dinklage, CEO of Gold-Partner MyCRM GmbH:

"We don't have to ask SugarCRM when we customize the product, since we can open the engine hood ourselves and implement customer requirements directly without additional communication overhead towards the platform vendor."

The identified framework of intra-platform and inter-platform effects shows that open source licensing strategy has a variety of strategic implications far beyond the basic business model mechanics.

3.5 Summary

In summary this section presented the inter-connection between a company's open source licensing strategy and its business model. In the case of SugarCRM the licensing strategy is the key enabler for the company's hybrid OSS business model. SugarCRM separates components that it licenses under an OSS license from those that it puts under a proprietary license in a single code tree, and in this way manages to combine the benefits of open source licensing with those of a proprietary product-based business model. The market success proves SugarCRM right. Industry experts expect the firms revenue to exceed 100 million USD in 2014 [5] and the firm claims to be have more than 1.5 million users[6].

---

[5] http://www.crmswitch.com/crm-industry/sugarcrm-company-history/

[6] http://www.forbes.com/sites/tomtaulli/2014/06/07/sugarcrm-should-salesforce-com-be-worried/

The key take-away for deciders in software companies is that licensing parts of a software offering under and FOSS license can bring a variety of benefits like efficient software R&D by an open innovation community. Still it complicates making money out of the firm's offering. The presented hybrid approach provides a pragmatic solution to this challenge. When open source licenses are parts of a business model and change in either of it affects the other. Therefore the licensing strategy and the business model have to be developed jointly when defining a new offering for a software company.

3.6   References for chapter 3

Bonaccorsi, A., Giannangeli, S. and Rossi, C. (2006), "Entry Strategies Under Competing Standards: Hybrid Business Models in the Open Source Software Industry", *Management Science*, Vol. 52 No. 7, pp. 1085–1098.

Carver, B.W. (2005), "Share and Share Alike: Understanding and Enforcing Open Source and Free Software Licenses", *Berkeley Technology Law Journal*, Vol. 20 No. 1, pp. 443–481.

Hecker, F. (1999), "Setting up shop: The business of open-source software. Software, IEEE", *Software, IEEE (Software, IEEE)*, Vol. 16 No. 1, pp. 45–51.

Lindman, J., Rossi, M. and Puustell, A. (2011), "Matching Open Source Software Licenses with Corresponding Business Models. Software, IEEE", *Software, IEEE (Software, IEEE)*, Vol. 28 No. 4, pp. 31–35.

Osterwalder, A. (2004), "The Business Model Ontology. A Proposition in a Design Science Approach", Dissertation, École des Hautes Études Commerciales, Université de Lausanne, Lausanne, 2004.

Popp, K.M. (2011), "Software Industry Business Models. Software, IEEE", *Software, IEEE (Software, IEEE)*, Vol. 28 No. 4, pp. 26–30.

Raymond, E.S. (2001), *The cathedral and the bazaar: Musings on Linux and Open Source by an accidental revolutionary,* Rev. ed., O'Reilly, Cambridge, Mass.

Riehle, D. (2012), "The single-vendor commercial open course business model", *Information Systems and e-Business Management,* Vol. 10 No. 1, pp. 5–17.

Waltl, J., Henkel, J. and Baldwin, C.Y. (2012), "IP Modularity in Software Ecosystems: How SugarCRM's IP and Business Model Shape Its Product Architecture. Software Business", in Cusumano, M.A., Iyer, B., Venkatraman, N., Aalst, W., Mylopoulos, J., Rosemann, M., Shaw, M.J. and Szyperski, C. (Eds.), *Lecture Notes in Business Information Processing,* Vol. 114, Springer Berlin Heidelberg, pp. 94–106.

Weill, P., Malone, T.W., D'Urso, V.T., Herman, G. and Woerner, S. (2005), "Do Some Business Models Perform Better than Others? A Study of the 1000 Largest US Firms".

West, J. (2003), "How Open Is Open Enough? Melding Proprietary and Open Source Platform Strategies", *Research Policy,* Vol. 32 No. 7, pp. 1259–1285.

4. Mergers and Acquisitions: Dealing with open source software in due diligence

Dr. Karl Michael Popp, SAP SE

In the process of acquiring companies a due diligence is executed to get detailed information about the company to be acquired. When acquiring software vendors, the due diligence of intellectual property rights is an important activity. The intellectual property rights in possession of or used by the acquisition target are analysed in detail.

Besides other types of third party software, open source software is in widespread use in commercial hardware and software products, since it is cheap and easily available. Open source software is intellectual property held by somebody in the open source community or by another software vendor. If the software vendor uses open source software in its products, the usage rights for that open source software have to be analyzed.

Open source software has rights and obligations that are defined within the open source license terms. These terms have to be checked and adhered to for avoiding certain risks of using open source software in commercial products.

Since software is becoming part of an increasing number of hardware products via embedded systems, too, the software-related due diligence activities get much more important for companies of industries like manufacturing and retail. Just think about the mobile applications that are available today for companies of almost all industries and about the role of software on devices in the internet of things.

To understand how open source is analyzed and in which context, it is important to know about intellectual property due diligence.

4.1   Introduction to intellectual property due diligence

In a knowledge-heavy industry, like the software industry, the utilization of intellectual property is often the core business. The monetization of that intellectual property must be preceded by the creation and protection of intellectual property (IP). So the takeover of such a company is driven by due diligence of intellectual property. You have to devote special attention and care to this topic.

In the software industry intellectual property is often the most important asset of a company. Besides employees and intellectual property there often are no other significant assets or means of production. But how is intellectual property generated and leveraged in the software industry?

4.2   Sources and usage of intellectual property rights in the software industry

To leverage IP for a company, IP to be owned by the company can be created or IP owned by other companies can be used or acquired. In software companies, products are created by own staff (employees) and contracted service providers (suppliers of services). Together with IP owned by other companies, like OEM software, freeware and open source software, this usually leads to a mix of components in a software product (Figure 13).

Example

To provide you with pragmatic knowledge, here are some numbers i met in practice. On average, based on my experience, a software product contains between 2-5 freeware components, 1-4 third party components and between 10 and fifty open source components. The maximum amount i experienced in large software solutions are: 10 freeware components, 150 third party components and 700 open source components.

Types of components of a software product

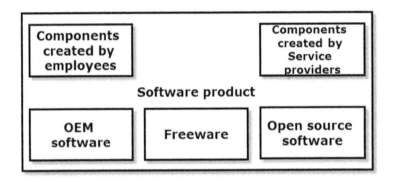

Figure 13: Types of components of a software product

A software vendor can also add new intellectual property to its portfolio by acquiring other companies (acquisition targets). In addition, the software vendor can apply for patents with patent authorities that might grant the patent to the software vendor (Figure 14).

Looking at intellectual property owned by other companies that the software vendor might use, four types are dominant in the software industry: patents, freeware, open source software and third party software. For the sake of simplicity, we will not cover third party content or services like e.g. database records or feeds, documents, news content or advertising.

Sources of intellectual property

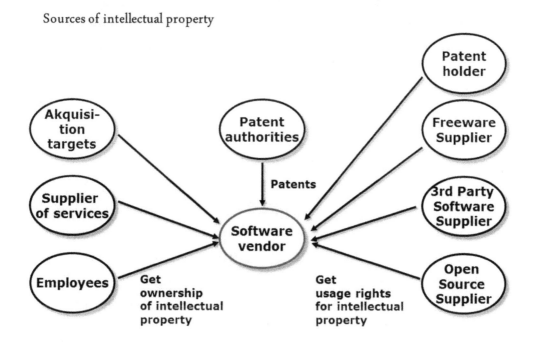

Figure 14: Sources of IP

When creating software for customers, software vendors often use (Figure 13):

☐ Software components created by the software vendor´s employees or by service providers,

☐ but also third party software components (OEM software, open source software, freeware).

Software components created by employees and service providers

The software vendor has to make sure to have ownership of the work results of employees and service providers working on the software. So the contracts with these two groups have to contain clauses that make sure the ownership of the work results is with the software vendor.

Why is this important for employees? Doesn't local law ensure anyway that the work results are owned by the software vendor? Actually, it depends on the intellectual property law and the work law of the country that the employees work in. In some countries companies own the work results of employees without specific clauses in the work contract, in some countries they don't. So you have to be aware and check this for each country you operate in.

Third party software components

The analysis of third party software usage is based on ownership and usage rights for these components like third party components with a commercial license, freeware and open source software components (see the right hand part of Figure 14). In addition, the software vendor might make use of patents held by other companies by getting a patent license.

Software is often licensed by a software vendor to customers for a license fee or offered as a cloud service. In order to assure that the software vendor can run such business with its customers, the ownership of and the usage rights for intellectual property have to be checked against the way the software vendor is utilizing the IP. Our special interest here will be on usage rights granted in the license of open source software.

Why is open source software important for due diligence?

As with other types of software, open source software comes with license terms. Some open source licenses carry restrictions and obligations that make commercial utilization hard, restricts it or makes it even impossible. To avoid the risk that the software under consideration cannot be commercialized, the licenses of all open source software components have to be diligently analysed.

4.3   Comprehensive IP due diligence

So what is important if you acquire a software company regarding intellectual property? In a holistic IP due diligence, the portfolio of intellectual property rights, the software vendor's relations with all sources of IP and the different types of intended utilization of intellectual property are examined.

With the intended acquisition of a software company the following views on intellectual property rights are relevant:

❑ The current state and future intentions for utilization of IP;

❑ Status and review of intellectual property rights and intellectual property usage rights at the target.

Let us start with the utilization first, because the utilization of IP will give us requirements for the review of IP rights and IP usage rights.

Review of the utilization of intellectual property

Utilization means the ways in which a software vendors wants to provide products and services and, if applicable, get revenues in return. Such ways might be direct sales or indirect sales to customers. Figure 15 shows examples of popular ways of utilization of IP in the software industry.

Example

Let us have a look at how a software vendor leverages intellectual property. In software sales, the obvious case is that the software vendor licenses software directly to the customer by granting usage rights. A second case is that the software vendor engages with a reseller. The software vendor grants sublicensing rights to the reseller and the reseller licenses the software to his customer by granting usage rights. In addition, the software vendor can grant licenses to patents held by the software vendor to patent licensees.

Utilization of intellectual property (Examples)

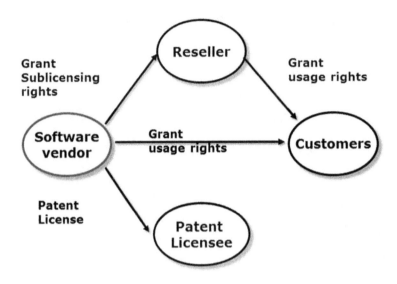

Figure 15: Utilization of IP

Utilizations and impact on IPR review

For all intended utilizations, the corresponding rights that are needed for all utilizations have to be available to the software vendor. That means that the software vendor has to have appropriate rights for each and every component of the software product to execute each and every intended utilization.

Example

An example for utilization might be that the software vendor sells the software to customers, runs the software for customers in the cloud and has resellers selling the software to customers.

Key questions Utilization

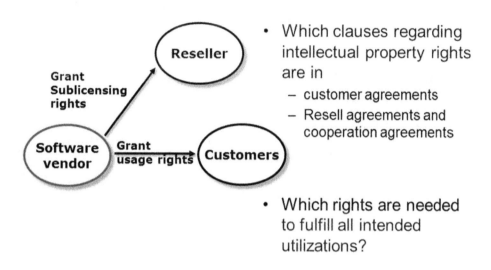

Copyright © 2012 Dr. Karl Popp

Figure 16: Key questions on IP utilization

Example

As an example, to establish resell relationships with partners, the software vendor has to be able to grant sublicensing rights to the resell partners. If the software product to be resold contains open source software, the software vendor needs sublicensing rights for the included open source software components, too.

What the utilization means with regard to open source software used

With open source software, you have to look at two things: rights and obligations. In our example the software vendor wants to grant usage rights and sublicensing rights to customers and resellers respectively.

If the software product contains open source software, the license coming with the open source software must not be in conflict with any of the utilizations planned. If there is a conflict, the intended utilization is not allowed. If and how that situation can be changed will be discussed later.

In addition, the open source software comes with obligations, which might also be in conflict with

☐ the IP strategy of the software vendor or

☐ the business model of the software vendor.

So important requirements for the review of open source licenses come from the utilizations.

Example

An example for utilization might be that the software vendor sells the software to customers, runs the software for customers in the cloud and has resellers selling the software to customers.

In this example, the software vendor has to make sure that the open source licenses allow that the software vendor sells the software to customers, runs the software for customers in the cloud and has resellers selling the software to customers.

The next step is to find the open source software components used as part of the review of status and usage of IP rights.

Review of own intellectual property and intellectual property used

Here you examine how intellectual property was created, acquired or licensed in the software company along the following questions:

☐ Has the software vendor sufficiently taken measures that work results of employees and service providers are IP of the target?

❏ Which patents, trademarks, copyrights, title protection and subsidiary measures exist and have been taken by the software vendor?

❏ Which clauses regarding intellectual property rights exist in customer contracts and cooperation agreements to ensure that none of the software vendor´s intellectual property rights or trade secrets are "lost"?

❏ Which third party intellectual property (e.g. Open Source Software) was and is used by the target and does the target have the appropriate usage rights matching the utilizations?

Key questions Sources

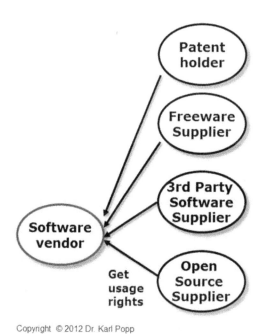

• Which third party intellectual property was and is used by the software vendor?

• Does the software vendor have the appropriate usage rights?

Figure 17: Key questions on IP sources (supplier relationships)

For each of its supplier relationships, the software vendor must ensure that it

❐ Either owns the intellectual property, which he uses or

❐ has sufficient rights to use third-party intellectual property.

Usage rights of third party intellectual property rights are e.g.:

❐ Licenses for patents held by other companies,

❐ Rights to use software components owned by other companies, including redistributables,

❐ Rights to use open source and freeware, which usually are available under open source and freeware licenses.

4.4 Best practice for open source review in IP due diligence

You can only provide open source software to customers if you comply with the corresponding license terms. This is why you have to identify and review each and every piece of open source software that is used in commercial software. Three steps are best practice in the software industry:

❐ Automated detection and identification of open source software components and their licenses,

❐ License review and evaluation,

❐ Creation and execution of a remediation plan.

Automated identification of open source

In due diligence, open source scanners, like the ones from Black Duck Software are used to detect all open source software used by an acquisition target. Based on this scan, the corresponding open source licenses and an overview of license types have to be provided.

To avoid exposure to target IP, the scan is executed as a hosted scan at the scanning company. The target gives its source code under strict NDA to the scanning company. During this process, the acquiring company does never have access or visibility into the source code of the target.

Scanning for open source in due diligence

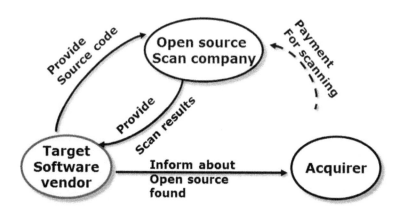

Figure 18: Key questions on IP sources (supplier relationships)

The scan is executed and the resulting reports are presented to the target. The target discusses the scan results with the acquiring company during due diligence.

License review and evaluation

Each license type and license found in the scan has to be analyzed regarding rights and obligations. The rights are compared against the rights needed to allow all intended utilizations. The obligations are checked if they are in conflict with the intended utilizations and if the software vendor can and wants to adhere to the obligations stated in the open source license terms.

Sometimes, there are open source licenses that are in conflict with intended utilizations or with the open source strategy of the acquirer. Then a remediation plan has to be created and executed.

Example

An acquirer's corporate open source strategy might be that GPL licensed open source must not be used in commercial products. If a target uses GPL software in its offerings, this would be a violation of the acquirer's open source strategy. A remediation plan has to be created containing the replacement or removal of the GPL licenses open source component.

Remediation Plan

If the software contains an open source software and the license of that open source is in conflict with the utilization, this situation has to be changed. Under the assumption that the utilization cannot be changed, there are several options for remediation:

❏ **Replace** the open source software. This might be done by Substitution with a functionally equivalent open source software with a compliant license,

❏ **Remove** the open source software. Especially if the open source software is used for building the software, but is not needed as part of the executable, it can be removed from the software product without a replacement.

❏ **Change the license terms**. Get a license for that open source software with different license terms, e.g.

   ❏ A different open source license in a case where an open source component has several, different open source license terms (dual licensing or multilicense strategies).

- ❐ A commercial license from the copyright holder of the open source software. From my experience, this was possible in just a few cases.

- ❐ A commercial license from companies specialized in offering commercial licenses for open source software. Some commercial software vendors offer commercial licenses for open source products. This is a popular case with dual licencing strategies for open source software.

The execution of the remediation plan can take place before or after the close of the deal. As soon as each license that conflicts with the utilization is removed, replaced or its license terms are changed, the utilization is possible.

K.M.Popp (ed.), Best practices for commercial use of open source software

5. Tools for Open Source Success

Bill Weinberg, Senior Director, Open Source Strategy – Black Duck Software

Greg Olsen, Senior Director, Governance Consulting – Black Duck Software

Much has been written regarding the open source development model and the dynamics of open source communities. Equally important are modes of using open source by different types organizations, best practices that govern use of code from open source projects and contributions to those projects, and ways to automate use and governance of open source software.

While the title of this chapter targets tooling, it is first essential to examine and understand requirements for and the context of automating open source practices, policies and procedures.

Figure 19: The Elements of an Open Source Strategy

5.1   Open Source Strategy

In the Black Duck Consulting practice, we are often asked to help organizations create strategies for optimizing returns on investment (ROI) in open source software. Those investments typically begin with consumption of open source software (OSS) but also encompass community participation and legal and business considerations, and can ultimately extend to building entire businesses on or around open source technology.

Agreeing upon an open source strategy is an essential first step to enhancing ROI from open source, on a par with having an overall business strategy. At the lowest level, strategy drives tactical concerns, in particular, use cases. Ultimately, companies wishing to monetize open source look to one of four basic business models based on open source software:

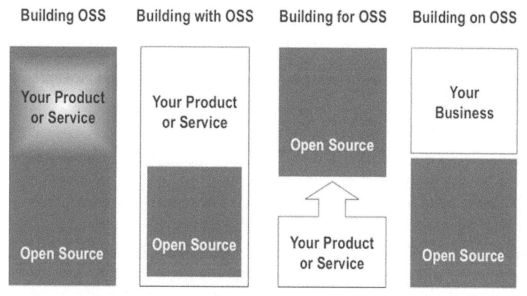

Figure 20: Core Open Source Business Models / Use Cases

Building OSS

The most basic (and most challenging) model involves creating and commercializing open source software for direct return. This approach can entail building platforms, middleware or applications as open source, for use in intelligent and mobile devices, on the desktop, in the data center and/or in the cloud – all as open source.

Building with OSS

The model is prevalent with device manufacturers (OEMs) and software vendors (ISVs) who typically use OSS to provide core functionality for their wares from several million projects and development communities. Examples include building network devices with embedded Linux, handsets and tablets with Android, and applications using frameworks, databases and other components like Qt, Node.js, Spring, PostgreSQL, CouchDB and myriad others.

Building for OSS

This model entails supplying training, documentation, tools, and support for existing open source technologies. Practitioners include distribution suppliers like Red Hat and HortonWorks, and also companies like Black Duck Software.

Building on OSS

This final model applies to technology companies and also to enterprise and IT organizations in small and medium sized businesses. *Building on OSS* means running your company with OSS for CRM, accounting, engineering, marketing – any and all business critical operations.

The above four paradigms address strategy – the devil, of course, is in the details, especially in terms of monetization. These models are not mutually exclusive; indeed many companies employ a combination of the four in their day-to-day business. What is most important is having a clear understanding of your OSS Strategy as you take on the challenge of Open Source Governance.

5.2   Open Source Governance

Open source governance comprises the policies, processes, procedures and also tradition and culture that surround the creation, development, deployment and maintenance of open source software (OSS). Many treatises focus on the governance of open source projects and the communities that arise around them. Here, instead, we examine governance as applied to OSS as consumed, contributed to, (re)distributed and also produced by commercial and governmental organizations, and focus on tools that facilitate these activities.

In this vein, open source governance is part of the broader category of *IT governance* which, according to the IT Governance Institute, helps ensure that IT supports business goals, maximizes business investment in IT and appropriately manages IT-related risks and opportunities.

The Need for Governance

For many IT, product development and services organizations, the acquisition of open source software has been largely organic and uncontrolled. Individual developers have enjoyed the freedom of searching the abundance of OSS code available on the Internet and used it without a formal acquisition process. However, as organizations increasingly rely on open source for business-critical applications, and OSS has grown to comprise a substantive portion of deployed code, the need for open source governance has evolved from a nicety into an imperative.

A decade ago, technology companies were the first to invest in tools for open source governance. Software vendors, device manufacturers (OEMs) and semiconductor suppliers were among the first to leverage OSS commercially and also the first to be concerned about how compliance with open source licenses might impact their control over technology and intellectual property portfolios.

More recently, enterprise IT (EIT) organizations began taking an interest in governance as well. While not usually redistributing OSS code (and thereby avoiding most open source license compliance requirements), EIT organizations today find themselves developing applications that are both internal and client-facing. They worry about compliance requirements that can accompany provision of services using OSS technologies, especially in the cloud. The primary concern of most EIT organizations with regard to OSS is software and information security; in particular, their focus is on the ability to identify and track software vulnerabilities and reliably manage their remediation. Some organizations also seek to be prepared for IP scrutiny that accompanies mergers and acquisitions.

Another key driver in formalizing open source governance in EIT is the need to comply with regulatory compliance regimes. Foremost among these are the Sarbanes-Oxley Act of 2002, a US federal law. These regimes and others require certification of proper financial procedures and controls in place, including the ability to verify ownership of material assets and assure information security. Lack of procedures to ensure compliance with open source licenses can run afoul of Sarbanes-Oxley in particular, because it would indicate an inability to verify provenance, ownership and proper use of intellectual property.

5.3   Open Source Policy and Procedures

While most of today's software managers are aware of the legal risks (e.g., license compliance) and the operational risks (e.g., compatibility requirements, security vulnerabilities, maintenance and support, etc.) that accompany use of open source, they also understand that the benefits of OSS far outweigh these concerns. As such, creating an open source software policy is a strategic imperative for organizations consuming, contributing to and producing open source software.

A policy is a set of rules and guidelines for using and managing OSS in your organization. To be effective, such a policy should cover all essential aspects of managing OSS, yet also be succinct and easily understood (otherwise no one will read it, much less follow it). A good rule of thumb is that OSS policies should be five pages or less, and realistically reflect the way software is developed and delivered in your company. Large organizations and those subject to compliance regimes often chose to cast their OSS policy into two documents:

❑ A simple, high level policy statement suitable for compliance verification, and

❑ A guidelines document containing the more detailed rules for use and management of OSS.

These policy documents must provide clear guidance and identification of responsibilities for all aspects of OSS use and management including:

❑ OSS discovery and evaluation,

❑ OSS review and approval,

❑ Commercial acquisition of OSS,

❑ OSS code management,

❑ OSS maintenance and support,

❑ OSS audit and compliance,

❑ OSS community participation,

❑ OSS governance program management.

A policy document provides the guidance, but effective OSS Governance is accomplished through a set of procedures that ensure that the guidance is consistently followed on a day-to-day basis. These procedures must document all tasks that must be performed and responsible parties or roles for their correct implementation.

In our experience at Black Duck Consulting, the two most important success factors in OSS governance implementation are that these procedures be well integrated with the existing software development processes of the organization, and that they be as efficient as possible, minimizing delay and overhead. One of the best ways to accomplish the latter is through automation of the governance procedures.

5.4 Open Source Logistics – Automating Governance

The concept of logistics is part of the lexicon of business planning. At its core is the idea that complexity does not inevitably lead to chaos, as long as there exists a coherent flow of dependencies among data, people, and things.

OSS Logistics provides organizations with systematic control over integration of open source into development and deployment of software and services:

CHOOSE SCAN APPROVE INVENTORY SECURE DELIVER

Figure 21: Phases of Open Source Logistics

☐ **Discovery and Selection**: Choosing the most appropriate, mature and functional open source code to meet an organization's needs.

☐ **Scanning**: Parsing a company code base for licenses, provenance, versions and risk profiles, across all phases of the software life cycle, in both traditional waterfall-based and agile / continuous delivery models.

☐ **Approval**: Approve code automatically with built-in policies and workflows.

☐ **Inventory and Tracking**: Documenting where open source is used in an organization and which code and versions are integrated and deployed.

☐ **Security**: Cataloguing vulnerabilities in open source code across organization software portfolios and facilitating remediation.

❑ **Delivery**: products and code confidently throughout the supply chain and to end users.

Types of Governance Tools

The evolution of enterprise-grade governance tools has greatly accelerated adoption of open source software, especially in enterprise settings. Most organizations begin adoption of open source with "organic" discovery and selection of open source software components by individual developers. When the need for open source management arises, the first tooling is typically an ad hoc mishmash of hardcopy notebooks, spreadsheets and shell scripts built on command line utilities like find, grep and awk.

Let's briefly examine the various types of tools available today, as both commercial and community offerings:

❑ **Discovery/Selection** – tools to help developers find appropriate open source project code, to vet its attributes (e.g., rates of release and commits over time), and also to build catalogs and white lists of code for approval (and black lists of code and licenses as well). Examples include Black Duck Code Center and OpenHub

❑ **Compliance** – the first step to successful open source compliance is to "know your code". To meet compliance requirements, tools must provide insight into the contents (bill of materials, BOM) of a code base or software portfolio, including the names, versions, licensing, provenance and security implications of code integrated therein. Compliance tools can also help build necessary documentation to support releases and checklists of disclosure requirements. Examples include Black Duck Protex, Black Duck Export, Fossology and the Binary Analysis Tool project.

❑ **Dependency Checkers** – Simply knowing which FOSS components are used in an application is usually not sufficient to inform efficient and correct compliance to the mix of open source licenses in todays software portfolios. Dependency checkers provide context to open source integration – how and where components, especially open source libraries are actually called and linked. Examples include Black Duck Protex and the Linux Foundation Dependency Tracker.

❏ **Code Sanitation** – utilities to cleanse source code of inappropriate language or proprietary information, such as the Linux Foundation Code Janitor.

❏ **Security Vulnerability Remediation** – With over 4,000 vulnerabilities reported for open source tools in 2014 alone, the focus on selection, detection and compliance has expanded to include securing open source components against emerging threats. A good example is the Black Duck Hub.

❏ **Supply Chain** – Software development organizations, in enterprise IT departments and at technology vendors, look to multiple sources for software. Today's development environment draws upon internally-developed code, open source project code, and also code supplied by third parties. That code can enter via commercial open source (e.g., Linux or Android distributions), and also as part of proprietary software libraries, toolkits and applications. Moreover, for comprehensive governance, companies need to look beyond their immediate supply chain, "upstream" and to realize that they may also be delivering software for "downstream" integration by customers and channel partners. Supply chain tools offer capabilities present in other governance tools (scanning, compliance, security, etc.) and formats such as the Software Package Data Exchange project SPDX standardize and ease communications between producers and consumers of software containing open source.

Governance Tools – Black Duck Offerings

Black Duck Software has set the standard for building and commercializing efficient, fast and robust tools to support open source governance:

Black Duck Code Center

Code Center supports an enterprise-wide framework that allows corporate decision makers to collaborate in managing software development policies. As part of the <u>Black Duck® Suite</u>, Code Center leverages comprehensive component metadata, including license information and security vulnerabilities, supplied by the <u>Black Duck® KnowledgeBase</u>. Code Center automates key governance processes:

- Searching for and selecting open source software (OSS),
- Obtaining approval for code use,
- Cataloging components for reuse and standardization.

Additionally, Code Center provides developers with visibility into component availability and desirability. Highly scalable, Code Center can support development teams of any size, whether co-located or geographically distributed, and can be deployed on premises or as software as a service (SaaS).

Code Center offers features for both OSS governance and security

- Daily security alerts with actionable information to help keep components secure.
- Security vulnerability detection with tuning options for low, medium and high threat ranking, and enabling companies to set policies and automate component approvals based on severity of vulnerabilities.
- Configurable and automated approval workflow.
- Deep License Data™ to uncover all license information, not just the declared license, enabling developers to make more informed component choices early in the SDLC.
- Catalog of approved components allowing tracking of where components are used across application portfolios.

❏ Component data, including associated metadata from Openhub.net, enabling informed component choices, including the ability to analyze component risk factors.

Black Duck PROTEX

Black Duck® Protex™ is the industry's leading solution for managing open source compliance. Protex integrates with existing development tools to automatically scan, discover and identify the origin and provenance of open source software, an integral step in the development process and essential for enforcing license compliance and corporate policy.

Protex helps organizations reduce business risk and complete software projects on-time and on-budget by automatically analyzing software contents, providing a bill of materials (BOM), uncovering potential risks early in the development cycle and identifying due diligence-related concerns well in advance of an audit. Protex Rapid ID™ automates the discovery and identification of open source code and Express Scan provides developers with a high-level snapshot of a code base up to four times faster than other code scanning solutions.

Protex is highly scalable and can support development teams of any size, whether co-located or geographically distributed, and can be deployed on premises or as software as a service (SaaS). Protex is also available as part of the Black Duck Suite, a comprehensive, automated OSS logistical approach to governance and compliance that integrates across the application development lifecycle.

Protex features:

❏ Fast, thorough discovery and identification of OSS and proprietary software components,

❏ Easy to use browser-based user interface,

❏ Comprehensive license management built upon the <u>Black Duck® KnowledgeBase™</u> ,

❏ Project review and approval automation with Code Label and BOM reports,

❏ Enterprise-class client-server architecture centralizes compliance data for shared access and collaboration.

The Black Duck Hub

The Hub is Black Duck's newest offering, leveraging the industry-recognized Black Duck KnowledgeBase (via the Cloud) and running on-premises in a lightweight web-based tool.

Use the Black Duck Hub to:

❏ Scan code to identify specific open source in use,

❏ Automatically map known vulnerabilities to open source components in use,

❏ Triage – assess risk and prioritize vulnerabilities,

❏ Schedule and track remediation,

❏ Identify licenses and community activity.

The Black Duck Hub continuously scans organization code bases for newly introduced open source, and helps manage security vulnerabilities before they become problems. The Black Duck Hub helps development teams review and prioritize vulnerabilities, assign remediation dates, and track closure. The Hub automatically monitors for new vulnerabilities reported against open source libraries used in applications and platforms, facilitating quick response as newly vulnerabilities surface.

The Black Duck Hub features;

☐ **Rapid Scanning** – Light weight, rapid identification of open source libraries, versions, license, and community activity.

☐ **Mapping Known Security Vulnerabilities** – Identify known vulnerabilities associated with open source in use and use vulnerability intelligence to prioritize and assign remediation dates.

☐ **Remediation Tracking** – Track planned and actual remediation dates for vulnerabilities within individual projects. Report output in CSV format supports importing to the reporting tool of your choice.

☐ **Risk Assessment Summary** – Review a dashboard of risk assessment in a straightforward user interface to maintain a pulse on security, community, and licensing risks. Drill down on vulnerability data to understand details associated with vulnerabilities within projects.

☐ **Black Duck KnowledgeBase** – Search the world's most comprehensive open source KnowledgeBase for accurate discovery, identification and vulnerability mapping of the open source in use within your projects.

☐ **Bills of Materials (BOMs)** – Create editable open source BOMs, with ability to adjust automated open source software libraries identified and add manual identifications.

☐ **Integrations** – Connect to continuous integration workflows using the Jenkins plugin to scan, discover, and auto-populate an open source BOM. Use the onboarding tool to auto-create projects.

Black Duck KnowledgeBase

The Black Duck® KnowledgeBase™ is the industry's most comprehensive database of open source project information, including in-depth metadata covering licensing and security attributes of millions of open source code bases. Since 2003, Black Duck crawlers have continuously searched the Internet for information on open source and downloadable code, making the KnowledgeBase an integral and unique asset that differentiates Black Duck products and services.

The KnowledgeBase helps developers find code and components, comprising

❒ Information on 1.1 million projects from over 8,500 sites across more than 350 billion lines of code

❒ Attributes of more than 2,400 unique software licenses (both OSI-recognized and self-styled FOSS licenses) including the full license text and dozens of encoded attributes and obligations for each license

❒ Detailed data on more than 69,000 security vulnerabilities, updated hourly

The Black Duck KnowledgeBase is continuously updated with thousands of new projects on a regular basis, and even includes information code and components from sources no longer available on the Internet.

Black Duck employs a team of developers, affectionately referred to as "spiders," dedicated to maintaining the KnowledgeBase, along with supporting the technology infrastructure and processes that have been developed over the course of many years.

Black Duck products leverage the KnowledgeBase for:

❒ Deep License Data™ that identifies "embedded licenses" to help organizations trust the use of thousands of projects with no declared license. Deep License Data also exposes those projects with no license data, generally determined to carry a high risk profile.

❒ Code search, scanning and analysis

❒ Comparing code fragments, source files, fully-formed components and binary files including executable files, static or dynamic libraries, images, icons, sound files, font files, logo files and archive files

- ❐ Ongoing, automated license compatibility notification

- ❐ Cataloging the origin and provenance of code

- ❐ Supporting custom code printing to allow addition of internally developed or third-party licensed code

- ❐ Quickly finding and identifying encryption software to automatically determine the applicable export rules for "crypto" elements

Black Duck Open Hub

The Black Duck Open Hub (www.openhub.net, formerlyOhloh.net) is an online community-based public directory of free and open source software (FOSS). The Open Hub offers analytics and search capabilities for discovering, evaluating, tracking, and comparing open source code and projects. The site also includes the Open Hub Code Search (code.openhub.net), a powerful free code search engine indexing over 21,000,000,000 lines of open source code from projects listed on the Black Duck Open Hub.

The Open Hub is crowd-curated and editable by all registered users, like a wiki. Anyone with an interest in FOSS is welcome to join, add new projects, and make corrections to existing project pages. This public review helps to make the Black Duck Open Hub one of the largest, most accurate, and up-to-date FOSS software directories available. Black Duck encourage contributors to join the Open Hub and claim their commits on existing projects and add projects not yet on the site. By doing so, Open Hub users can assemble a complete profile of all their FOSS code contributions.

The Open Hub is not a forge — it does not host projects and code. Rather, the Open Hub is a directory and community, offering analytics and search services and tools. By connecting to project source code repositories, analyzing both the code's history and ongoing updates, and attributing those updates to specific contributors, the Black Duck Open Hub can provide reports about the composition and activity of project code bases and aggregate this data to track the changing demographics of the FOSS world.

Black Duck Vulnerability Plug-in for Jenkins

The Jenkins platform is the leading open source continuous integration (CI) server built with Java. It provides over 400 plugins to support building and testing virtually any project. It supports SCM tools including Subversion, GIT, Mercurial, Perforce, RTC, Apache ant and Apache Maven projects as well as shell scripts and Windows batch commands.

Black Duck's Vulnerability Plug-in for Jenkins works by leveraging the Black Duck KnowledgeBase and by extracting dependency data from Jenkins builds. It streamlines discovery of specific versions of open source software in use, and then cross-references those open source components with databases of catalogued vulnerabilities associated with those modules. The plug-in minimizes the need for exhaustive inspection (human intervention) and doesn't slow down daily (or hourly) builds and associated Agile sprints. Developers can export PDF reports listing the vulnerabilities and share them with security teams and architects for easy collaboration and remediation.

Other Jenkins Integrations

Black Duck also offers Jenkins integrations with tools from the Black Duck Suite:

- ☐ **Code Center** – Easily access a build in Jenkins and compare the build Bill Of Materials (BOM) against the Black Duck Code Center application BOM. You'll then have the ability to automatically create component requests for the application with any new dependencies found in the build.

- ☐ **Protex** – The Protex Jenkins Plug-in provides the ability to configure Jenkins builds to either point to an existing Protex project or create a new project for the bulid. The plug-in will also initiate a scan of the project code and can then be set to "Fail" the build if any pending ID's or license conflicts are found during the scan.

Other Open Source Governance Tools

The following tools and related projects are available from a range of community sites and organizations:

BAT – The Binary Analysis Tool

Most governance tools scan the source code of open source software and of software that integrates FOSS. However, with software delivered by third parties and in other scenarios, source code is not always immediately available or binary files in question only contain imperfect subsets of FOSS called out in reports and manifests. In these cases, open source management teams need a "can opener" to peek inside executables and other binary assets (blobs) to discover which (if any) open source code is deployed within.

The Binary Analysis Tool (BAT) lets FOSS management teams look inside binary code, find compliance issues, and reduce uncertainty when deploying Free and Open Source Software. BAT is a modular framework that assists compliance and due diligence activities and is available for free under the Apache license.

BAT can open more than 30 types of compressed files, file systems and media files, search for Linux kernel and BusyBox issues, identify dynamically linked libraries and explore ELF files, Android Dalvik and Java class files using a database of information extracted from source code.

Fossology

Fossology.org set out to build a community to facilitate the study of Free and Open Source Software by providing free and open source data analysis tools. Fossology later evolved to comprise a set of tools to assist in open source governance, predominantly for scanning files for licenses and copyrights. In particular, Fossology supports upload of code to web/cloud-hosted utilities, scanning for licenses, copyrights and other metadata, and a report generation framework for use with custom workflows.

Linux Foundation Tools

Since its founding, the Linux Foundation has initiated the creation of several tools to facilitate open source code management and governance. These tools are licensed under the MIT license, and the Linux Foundation encourages community involvement in their evolution.

❏ **FOSS BarCode Tracker** – this tool simplifies the way FOSS components are tracked and reported in a commercial product. The tool allows companies to generate a custom QR code for each product containing FOSS. The QR code contains important information on the FOSS stack contained in a product, such as component names, version numbers, license information and links to download the source code, among other details.

❏ **Dependency Checker** – this tool identifies source code combinations at the dynamic and static link levels and provides a license policy framework to enable FOSS Compliance Officers to define combinations of licenses and linkage methods that are to be flagged for investigation or remediation if encountered by the tool

❏ **Code Janitor** – this tool provides linguistic review capabilities to ensure that developers did not leave comments in the source code about future products, product code names, mention of competitors, etc. The tool maintains a database of target keywords to identify when scanning source code to provide assurances that source code comments are sanitized and ready for public consumption

SPDX

The Software Package Data Exchange project (http://spdx.org/ , SPDX®) is creating a standard format for communicating the components, licenses and copyrights associated with a software package.

The SPDX standard helps facilitate compliance with free and open source software licenses by standardizing the way license information is shared across the software supply chain. SPDX reduces redundant work by providing a common format for companies and communities to share important data about software licenses and copyrights, thereby streamlining and improving compliance.

The SPDX specification is developed by the SPDX workgroup, which is hosted by the Linux Foundation. The grass-roots effort includes representatives from more than 20 organizations—software, systems and tool vendors, foundations and systems integrators – all committed to creating a standard for software package data exchange formats.

Black Duck Support of SPDX

Black Duck has been instrumental in developing SPDX through participation in the SPDX workgroup, including

❐ Chairing the SPDX workgroup

❐ Active participation in the three SPDX teams: Technical, Business and Legal

❐ Authoring the first <u>SPDX whitepaper</u>

❐ Developing and evolving the structure of spdx.org and supporting the SPDX beta process

❐ Implementing SPDX software BOM in the <u>Black Duck® Suite</u> as a standard feature

Stay tuned for additional SPDX integration and support by Black Duck in upcoming products and services for the software supply chain.

6. Creating developer value from open source software management

Robert Reiz, VersionEye

Software developers are using open source software for several reasons like maturity, security and because it is free of charge. Although open source components are typically of high maturity and security the question arises how to manage them as soon as they are part of a commercial product.

6.1 How companies manage open source components as part of software products

Let us have a look how open source components are managed in development operations of a typical software vendor. Open source components, like other software components, are integrated into a software product. While proprietary components are maintained by a developer and commercial third party components like OEM software are maintained by the supplier, open source components are often maintained by the open source community.

If developers are using open source components, these are integrated into source code and binary repositories. Updates of these open source components are now within the responsibility of a developer.

Keeping the open source component up-to-date means following or being part of the activities of the open source community around that specific component. If only a few open source components are used, this is an easy task.

Maintenance and support for components of a software product is usually done by

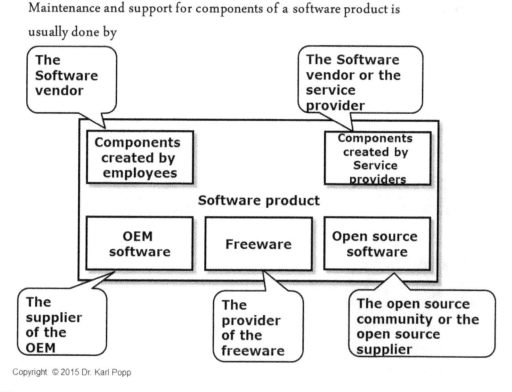

Figure 22: Key questions on IP sources (supplier relationships)

On average, software products usually contain between a few and a few hundred open source components. The complexity gets even worse when we consider the fact that open source components themselves often contain numerous other open source components.

While it is easy for a developer to follow the community for one component, it is hard to follow the communities of dozens of open source components and getting notice of updated and improved versions of open source components. So the usage of numerous open source components leads to high effort maintenance work for developers which lowers productivity.

In addition, this situation results in many challenges of including "old" versions of open source components in software products, which are outlined in the next section.

6.2   What is the impact of using "old" versions of open source components?

Software developers don't release new versions just for fun. Releasing a new version is always a lot of work. The documentation needs to be updated, new binaries or bundles need to be packaged and published to repository servers such as NRMRegistry, RubyGems or Maven Central. And finally the community has to be informed somehow.

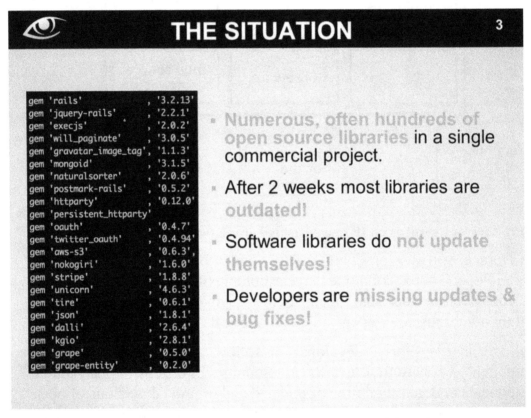

Figure 23: Impact of using open source libraries in commercial projects
The most important reasons for a new version are: new functionalities, bug fixes, security vulnerability fixes and keeping compatibility with newer versions of other open source components. Every time a new version for an open source library gets released for one of the reasons above. So it is paramount for applications developers to catch up with the

newest versions and keep the dependencies to and between open sources up-to-date.

Missing bug fixes

The open source community is continuously updating and improving quality of open source components. This is one of the main reasons why people use open source software.

So if you use an old version of an open source component you might lose the bug fixing power of the community. The key question remains how to get informed about updates of open source components without following each community for each open source component.

Missing security vulnerability fixes

Fixing security vulnerabilities of commercial and open source components is a key activity in the software industry. Frequently used open source components often also have a high frequency of security related updates. Hackers are following security related incidents and are trying to exploit vulnerabililties that might exist in open source software that has not been updated. If a developer misses an update, he exposes his products and their customers to a hacker attack, since the hackers know about this vulnerability that hasn´t been fixed in an old version of the software.

Dependencies and potential incompatibilities

It might be that a software team has to update component A to the newest version because some outside APIs changed. A good example for this is the transition from country specific Bank transactions to the European standard IBAN & BIC.

If component A is used for Bank transactions and it has to be updated to the next major version it is very likely that the transitive dependencies of component A have to be updated, too. If an application has transitive dependencies from A, the new version of component A will not work with the application. This is a pretty common case for issues during a software development cycle.

Since popular open source components have many transitive dependencies, work on dependencies has to happen nearly every time with all major updates of Ruby on Rails, Spring, Hibernate and other open source components. Usually that leads to a refactoring because a high number of dependendent components have to be migrated to new major versions. These updates can be avoided by continuous updating. If developers get notified about new versions immediately they can update the open source components on-the-fly and do migrations inside of sprints.

6.3   Creating value for developers by continuously updating open source components

Following and identifying new or updated versions of open source components is requiring high efforts and tedious work. Short, agile development cycles demand a high rate of updates to software components and keep developers busy. So the focus of developer activity should not be on manually looking for updates to open source software. The activity of following open source updates and notifying the developer about updates can be automated and outsourced.

This is where VersionEye delivers its value to developers. VersionEye is a cloud service that will serve you with key information and updates about open source components. It will natively plug into your development environment and alert you to any updates of your open source components.

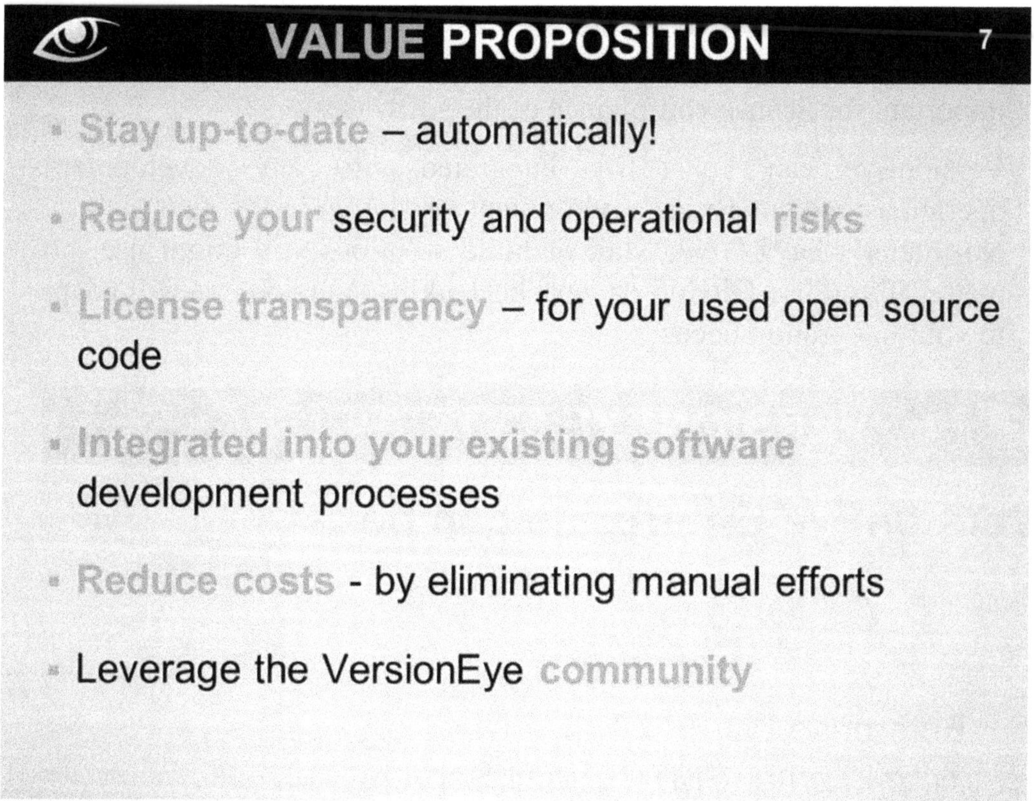

VALUE PROPOSITION   7

- Stay up-to-date – automatically!

- Reduce your security and operational risks

- License transparency – for your used open source code

- Integrated into your existing software development processes

- Reduce costs - by eliminating manual efforts

- Leverage the VersionEye community

Figure 24: Value propositions of VersionEye

Key value propositions of VersionEye

☐ Updates of the open source software are never missed, so the latest version of the open source software is always being used.

☐ Bugfixes are never missed: if there exists a newer version of the open source software, which is of higher quality and it contains less bugs, developers will get an alert immediately.

☐ Security vulnerability fixes are never missed. This is a very hot topic. Since not only developers are looking for fixing security vulnerabilities in products, but also hackers are interested in attacking these vulnerabilities.

❒ License information about the licenses of the open source libraries used is always transparent and can be easily reviewed. This is important for license compliance of the software.

❒ VersionEye can be easily integrated into any development operations and enterprise environment, as shown in the next picture. No matter what LDAP, Mail or build solutions you might use, no matter if you use GitHub or Apache Jenkins, VersionEye will adapt to your integration needs.

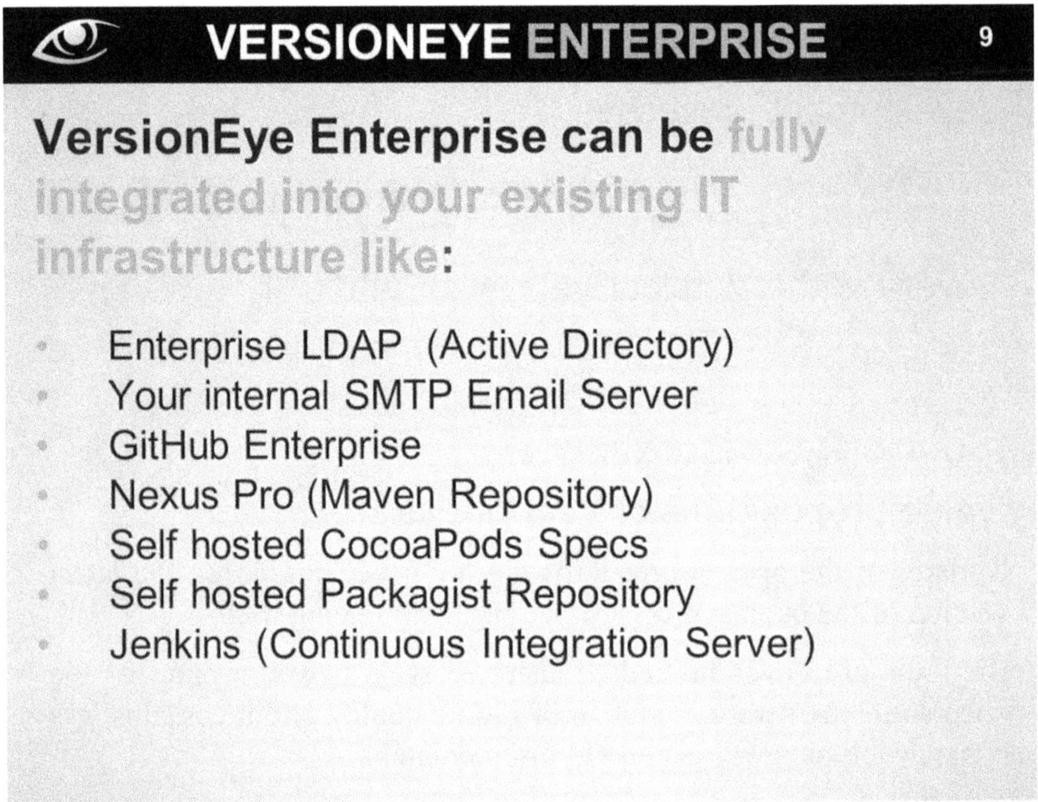

VERSIONEYE ENTERPRISE   9

VersionEye Enterprise can be fully integrated into your existing IT infrastructure like:

- Enterprise LDAP (Active Directory)
- Your internal SMTP Email Server
- GitHub Enterprise
- Nexus Pro (Maven Repository)
- Self hosted CocoaPods Specs
- Self hosted Packagist Repository
- Jenkins (Continuous Integration Server)

Figure 25: VersionEye integration advantages

❒ Detection vs. active support and value for developers. VersionEye alerts the developer within the development and build environment about updates. There is no need for developer education or complex processes.

❏ Manual, error-prone tasks are automated. Manual lookup of new versions by developers can be eliminated and with this you eliminate potential look-up errors as well.

Display of security vulnerabilities

Security vulnerabilities of components are automatically and instantly displayed as security alerts in the component list of your project.

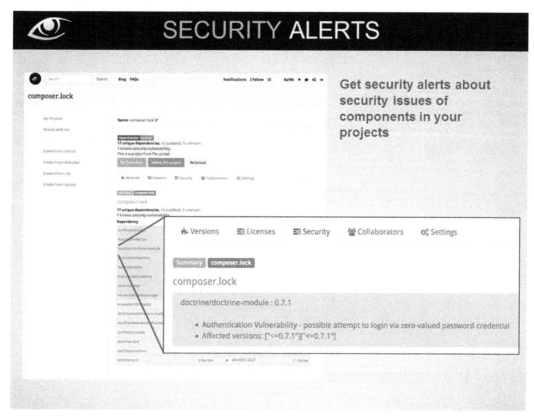

Figure 26: VersionEye security alerts

Leveraging License whitelists

If your company has a whitelist of open source licenses which are compliant with the company´s open source policy, you can use it to instantly display compliance with the license whitelist. Compliant licenses are displayed in green color.

So everytime a developer displays the project, he can immediately see if the licences of open source components are contained in the whitelist or not.

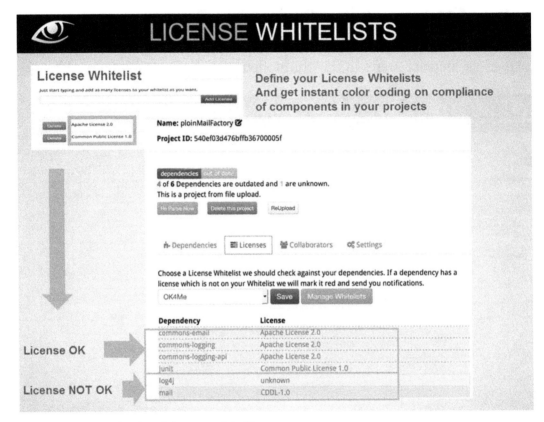

Figure 27: VersionEye License whitelists

Actively managing dependencies

Dependent components, which are not updated frequently, can cause severe issues in the software development cycle. VersionEye attacks this dependency issue by displaying the status of dependent components in your project.

All used components, which should be updated, are marked in red. So developers can instantly react to this situation and resolve it.

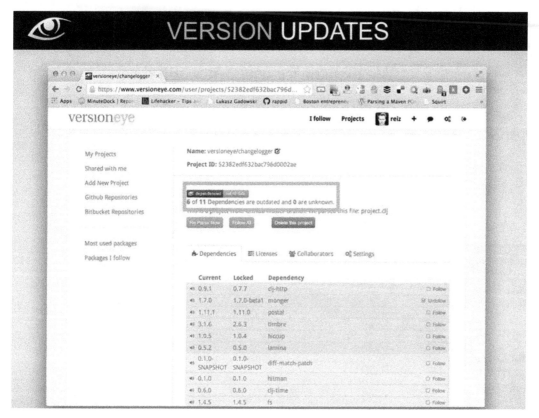

Figure 28: VersionEye Dependency management

Coverage of open source projects

But how can a single system provide such a service? There must be a myriad of open source libraries out there. How can a developer be sure that VersionEye monitors all the relevant libraries?

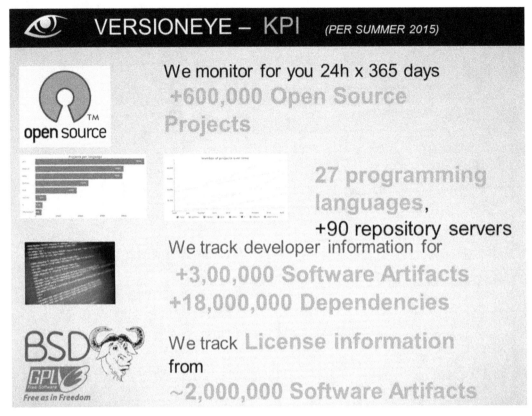

Figure 29: VersionEye KPIs

The answer is: VersionEye runs a crawling cluster in the cloud, similar to Google, but crawling is specialised on open source software libraries. The VersionEye crawlers are running continuously and they monitor currently more than half a million open source projects for you. The crawling framework covers Open Source projects from 27 programming languages on several repository servers. In total, more than 2 million open source software artifacts are covered.

VersionEye offers more than just alerts and updates on changed open source components. The collected open source meta data includes information about the projects such as version number, licenses, change-logs, descriptions, authors and many more. The VersionEye database stands out among the biggest databases about open source software.

Value of additional information about open source

Beyond crawling open source, aggregating open source information and alerting on updates the question remains how you pick the right piece of open source software for your product during development. You might want to choose an open source component that is frequently used and updated by the open source community.

Besides continuous updates, you can leverage VersionEye information to select the right open source component based on different attributes like the license type or a whitelist of allowed licenses in a software company.

With VersionEye, it is simple to choose the right open source component based on:

❏   frequency of usage in other products,

❏   update frequency,

❏   the age of the component,

❏   the license of the open source component.

6.4   Summary

Following and identifying new or updated versions of open source components is a high effort, error-prone and tedious work. The same is true for open source license information.

VersionEye solves this problem by providing automated lookups of open source library updates and licensing information for more than a quarter million open source libraries. Development operations can be simplified by integrating VersionEye into build processes. Developer productivity can be increased by replacing manual search and updates by automated alerting   and   updates.   Find   more   information   here: http://www.versioneye.com

7. Advertising

7.1 Book: Mergers and Acquisitions in the software industry

Karl Michael Popp, Ralf Meyer:
Mergers and Acquisitions in the software industry:
Foundations of due diligence
This book is about foundational methods for due diligence of software companies.
Topics covered in this book are: Business modeling, Foundations of due diligence, Foundations of M&A, impact of business models and revenue models on due diligence, impact of partner ecosystems on due diligence.

The book is available on Amazon (ISBN: 9783848221998), on iTunes and for Kindle. For more information see www.mergerduediligence.de

7.2 Book: Intellectual Property Modularity in Software Products and Software Platform Ecosystems

Josef Waltl:

Intellectual property modularity in software products and software platform ecosystems:

This book examines the impact of Intellectual Property (IP) modular architecture on software products and software platform ecosystems. The presented results are based on a detailed qualitative case study analysis of two software products and two software platforms and on a quantitative study of two software ecosystems.The results extend the existing literature on IP modularity by demonstrating a direct association between IP modular product or platform architecture and the related business models.

The book is available on Amazon (ISBN: 978-3732237937), on iTunes and for Kindle.

7.3   Book: Profit from Software Ecosystems

Karl Michael Popp, Ralf Meyer:

Profit from software ecosystems

Business Models, Ecosystems and Partnerships in the software industry

This book is about the mechanics of ecosystems and how to survive and generate revenue through ecosystems and software partnerships written by practitioners for software professionals. Topics covered in this book are: Economic foundations, value chains and business models in the software industry, Ecosystems and the available partnering models in the software industry as well as prominent examples from Google, Microsoft, SAP and others.

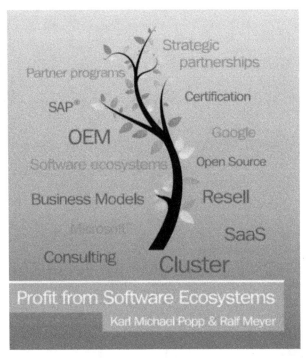

The book is available on Amazon (ISBN: 978-3842300514), on iTunes and for Kindle.

For more information see www.synomic.com/partnerbook

7.4   Open source best practices website

HTTP://OPENSOURCEBESTPRACTICES.NET/

On this website you will find best practices for:

- Open source licensing,
- Open source due diligence,
- Open source business models,
- Open source governance,
- Open source compliance tools,
- Open source developer tools,
- And Open source books, presentations and videos

HTTP://OPENSOURCEBESTPRACTICES.NET/

7.5   WWW.DRKARLPOPP.COM website

WWW.DRKARLPOPP.COM is your **one-stop-shop for wisdom about the software industry**. It covers topics like

- **Business Models in the software industry,**
- **Software Ecosystems,**
- **Mergers and Acquisitions in the software industry,**
- **Due Diligence and Post Merger Integration,**
- **Open Source Licensing and**
- **Partnerships in the software industry**

Get the latest books, e-books and videos about the software industry at WWW.DRKARLPOPP.COM.

7.1 Book: Partnering with SAP

Ralf Meyer:

Partnering with SAP:

Business Models for Software Companies

How can a software vendor leverage SAP for his business? This book provides answers and gives interested readers an overview of the multiple options to partner with SAP.

It is an excellent starting point for anybody in the software industry who wants to leverage the huge SAP ecosystem for their strategic growth plans and learn how to partner with SAP.

The book is available on Amazon (ISBN: 978-3837060553).

For more information see www.synomic.com/partnerbook

Synomic

Synomic www.synomic.com is a boutique management consultancy and was founded in 2006 by Software and SAP Ecosystem experts. Focus is on Alliance Management, Business Development and Corporate Development consulting including Go-to-Market (GTM) and the support of the Venture Capital funding process.

Tailored offerings address the specific needs of Software Companies:

- ❐ Leverage the huge SAP Ecosystem for GTM and business success
- ❐ Implement or improve a winning SAP Partnering Strategy
- ❐ Go-to-Market in Germany/Europe/USA with or without focus on the SAP Ecosystem
- ❐ Corporate development including the support for the Venture (VC) Funding process
- ❐ SAP and IT partnering know-how and best practices
- ❐ Support for marketing and sales (channel/direct)
- ❐ Coaching for teaming with SAP and other IT ecosystems

Benefits include

- ❐ More productive partnering & business relationships
- ❐ Increased focus on core competencies
- ❐ Quicker scaling of business with reduced overall costs and risk

Examples of Services

- ❐ Service SAP Ecosystem Strategy
    - ❐ Assessment and strategy development
    - ❐ Business and partnering models
    - ❐ Market and white space analysis

❏ Corporate Development
  ❏ Support of the venture capital (VC) funding process
  ❏ Go-to-market strategy development
  ❏ Interim Corporate Development
❏ Business Development
  ❏ Market and white space analysis including feasibility studies
  ❏ Support the implementation and execution of business plans
  ❏ Go-to-market in Germany including sales support
  ❏ Interims Business Development
❏ Synomic "Partner Incubator"
  ❏ Virtual presence @ SAP in Walldorf
  ❏ Orchestration of services provided by Synomic partners
  ❏ Business Start in Germany

Contact:

Synomic GmbH
Altrottstrasse 31
SAP Partner-Port
69190 Walldorf
info@synomic.com
Phone: +49-(0)6227-73-2455
Fax: +49-(0)6227-73-2459

8. Literature

[1]   J. Lerner and J. Tirole, "Economic Perspectives on Open Source," in *Perspectives on free and open source software*, vol. 15, J. Feller, B. Fitzgerald, S. Hissam, and K. Lakhani, Eds. MIT Press, 2005, pp. 47-78.

[2]   A. Deshpande and D. Riehle, "The Total Growth of Open Source," in *Open Source Development Communities and Quality*, 2008, vol. 275, no. 2006, pp. 197-209.

[3]   T. Jaeger, O. Koglin, T. Kreutzer, A. Metzger, and C. Schulz, "Die GPL kommentiert und erklärt," in *Die GPL kommentiert und erklärt*, Institut für Rechtsfragen der Freien und Open Source Software, O'Reilly, 2005, pp. 1-24.

[4]   A. Onetti and S. Verma, "Open Source Licensing and Business Models," *ICFAI Journal of Knowledge Management*, vol. VII, no. 1, pp. 68-95, 2009.

[5]   S. Krishnamurthy, "An Analysis of Open Source Business Models," in *Source*, vol. 54, no. February, J. Feller, B. Fitzgerald, S. A. Hissam, and K. R. Lakhani, Eds. The MIT Press, 2005, pp. 267-278.

[6]   K. Popp and R. Meyer, *Profit from Software Ecosystems: Business Models, Ecosystems and Partnerships in the Software Industry [Paperback]*. Books on Demand, 2010, p. 242.

[7]   M. Stürmer and T. Myrach, "Open source community building," *Lutterbeck Bernd et al Open Source Jahrbuch*, pp. 219–234, 2006.

[8]   L. Dahlander, M. G. Magnusson, Jürgen Bitzer, and Philipp J H Schröder, "Business Models and Community Relationships of

Open Source Software Firms," in *The Economics of Open Source Software Development*, Elsevier, 2006, pp. 111-130.

[9]   T. W. Malone et al., "Do Some Business Models Perform Better than Others?," *Social Science Research*, no. May, 2006.

[10]   J. Lindman and R. Rajala, "How Open Source Has Changed the Software Industry: Perspectives from Open Source Entrepreneurs," *Technology Innovation Management Review*, no. January, pp. 5-11, 2012.

[11]   J. Henkel, "Open source software from commercial firms–tools, complements, and collective invention," *Zeitschrift Für Betriebswirtschaft*, vol. 4, no. 4, pp. 1–23, 2004.

[12]   M. Välimäki, "Dual Licensing in Open Source Software Industry," *Business*, vol. 8, no. 1, pp. 63-75, 2003.

[13]   K. J. Bekkelund, "Succeeding with freemium," NTNU, 2010.

[14]   N. Pujol, "Freemium : attributes of an emerging business model," *Organization*, no. December, 2010.

[15]   A. I. Wasserman, "Building a Business on Open Source Software," in *Cases in Technological Entrepreneurship Converting Ideas into Value*, Edward Elgar, 2009.

[16]   D. Ascher, "Is Open Source Right for You?: A fictional case study of open source in a commercial software shop," *Queue*, vol. 2, no. 3, pp. 32-38, 2004.

[17]   M. A. Cusumano, *The Business of software*, vol. 44, no. 3. Free Press, 2004, pp. 15-18.

9. Index

Business models
and licensing strategy, 23, 31
commercial open source, 20, 25
contractor, 19
definition, 31
hybrid, 17, 20, 34
Inventor, 19
IP lessor, 19, 32
open source, 17

Companies
Black Duck Software, 52, 58, 64
Hortonworks, 58
InsignioCRM, 38
Jaspersoft, 10
MyCRM, 39
Red Hat, 10, 58
SugarCRM, 34
Synomic, 12
VersionEye, 80

Contracts
customer contracts, 51
NDA, 52

Development operations
build tools, 72, *82*
continuous updating, 79
Software Package Data
  Exchange standard, 74

Due diligence, 42
of intellectual property, 46

Intellectual property, 43
donation, 16
due diligence, 43, 46
homogeneity, 36
review of existing, 50
sources of, 43
strategy, 36
utilization, 47, 48

Laws
intellectual property law, 46
work law, 46

Network effects, 37

Open source
business models, 17, 37
commercial licensing, 22
commercial open source, 14
commercial services for, 21
community open source, 14, 33
compliance, 29, 60
dependency, 63
governance, 59
impact of updates, 76
maintenance, 76
management, 76
policy, 60
risk, 79

scanners, 52
strategy, 57
support for, 76
Updates, 76

Open source community
as supplier, 27
as supporter, 29

Open source components
Apache Ant, 72
Apache Jenkins, 72, *82*
Apache Maven, 72
Apache Maven Central, *78*
CouchDB, 58
GIT, 72
Hibernate, 80
Mercurial, 72
Node.js, 58
Perforce, 72
PostgreSQL, 58
Qt, 58
RTC, 72
Ruby on Rails, 80
Spring, 58, 80
Subversion, 72

Open source issues
dependencies, 79, 84
license compliance, 73
maintenance and support, 60
missing bug fixes, 79
security vulnerabilities, 60, 79

Open source license, 13
Apache, 33
BSD, 33
GNU Affero General Public
License, 35
GPL, 33, 54
MIT, 33
permissive license, 33
restrictive license, 33

Open source licensing
dual licensing, 20, 24, 54
remediation, 54
whitelist, 83

Open source projects
Apache, 10

Open source software
definition, 10

Open source tools
Black Duck Code Center, 65
Black Duck KnowledgeBase,
69
Black Duck Protex, 64
Linux Foundation Code
Janitor, 64
Linux Foundation
Dependency Tracker, 64
VersionEye, 80

Partner relationships
resell, 49

Proprietary software license,
  20, 32, 34

Third party software

as part of software products,
  77

in IP due diligence, 46

CPSIA information can be obtained
at www.ICGtesting.com
Printed in the USA
BVHW06s1709310518
517877BV00003B/45/P

9 783738 619096